Pull up a chair.
Take a taste.
Come join us.
Life is so endlessly delicious.
— *Ruth Reichl*

FOR GOODNESS SAKE

FOR GOODNESS SAKE

Plant-Based
Recipes from the
Spiral House Kitchen

Featuring Chef Diane Hagedorn

Photographs by Andrea Barrist Stern

Rafferty Rocks Press
Saugerties, New York

Copyright © 2016 by Rafferty Rocks Press
Sculpture copyright © 2000–2016 Tom Gottsleben

All Rights Reserved
Published by Rafferty Rocks Press, Saugerties, NY
Distributed by Book Publishing Company
    P.O. Box 99, Summertown TN, 38483
    Orders: 888.260.8458 | info@bookpubco.com

Library of Congress Cataloging-in-Publication Data
Rafferty Rocks Press
    For Goodness Sake: Plant-Based Recipes from the Spiral
    House Kitchen/Rafferty Rocks Press
            Pages cm
    Includes Index
1. Vegan cooking. 2. Plant-based cooking. 3. Vegetarian
    cooking. 4. Natural foods. 5. Organic foods.
TXU1964066

Hardcover ISBN: 978-1-57-067339-9

Book design: Ronnie Shushan
Photography and food styling: Andrea Barrist Stern
Editors: Andrea Barrist Stern and Ronnie Shushan

Additional photographs by Mick Hales (front endpaper
    and pages 2, 41, 69, 99, 125, 162, 219, 239, 260)
Phil Mansfield (pages 161 and 193)
Tom Gottsleben (pages 17 and 232)
Patty Livingston (page 170)
Anjali Bermain (pages 210–211)

Printed in the United States
First Printing, 2016

10 9 8 7 6 5 4 3 2 1

FSC
www.fsc.org
MIX
Paper from
responsible sources
FSC® C002589

The Forest Stewardship Council (FSC) was
created in 1993 to help consumers and
businesses identify products from well-managed
forests. FSC is an independent nonprofit
organization that sets standards by which forests
are certified, offering credible verification to
people who are buying wood and wood products.

For the animals: farm, domestic, wild . . . all of them, everywhere. May they delight in the pure joy that comes from walking free under the open sky with ample and healthy food to eat. May they experience the comfort of companionship with kindred souls that all living beings need. May they enjoy the mental stimulation their inquisitive, problem-solving minds require. May they find the peace that all of us were born to know.

CONTENTS

page 64

page 18

page 100

page 112

page 70

page 128

page 158

page 216

INTRODUCTION

Welcome to *For Goodness Sake,* a cookbook about food that is good for you, good for all living things, and good for the planet we call home. For Goodness Sake is more than a title; it's the central philosophy of this cookbook and the group that produced it, goodness being the value we aspire to bring to every part of our lives, from our actions and our relationships to the food we put into our bodies.

At its core, though, this is really a book about community. It addresses the things a group of professionals, friends, and artists who work together have learned about growing, preparing, preserving, and sharing the food we eat daily. Like an increasing number of people everywhere, many of us have turned to a plant-based diet for health reasons, as a doorway to what we see as a more compassionate lifestyle, and to minimize our footprints on the earth through our food-related choices.

The recipes are selected from the varied dishes that Chef Diane Hagedorn creates for us each day in the kitchen of the Spiral House, a unique stone structure based on sacred geometry that was designed by artist Tom Gottsleben. (Visit him at tomgottsleben.com to see his work.) Tom and his wife, Patty Livingston, have lived in New York's Hudson River Valley since the early 1980s on a property that was once a bluestone quarry. There, in the late 1990s, he designed and built the spiral structure, essentially sculpting a home on this land.

During the building process, and in the years since then, the couple assembled a small community of stoneworkers, artists, and writers who comprise Tom's sculpture crew, produce his publications, work on the many organic vegetable and flower gardens, and tend to the daily needs of such a large operation. At lunch, all are welcome to share the gourmet vegan meals created by Diane and her sous chef, Valerie Augustine.

Like so many creative individuals before her, Diane eventually gave in to Tom and Patty's coaxing to join the group full-time several years ago. The garden crew, Jane Polcovar and Sara Gast, were recruited to help prepare the food. Other lunch regulars include Andrea Barrist Stern, the head gardener, who is also a professional photographer; and Ronnie Shushan, an editor/designer working on a book about the creation of the Spiral House. In retrospect, it seems inevitable that this merry band would begin turning Diane's recipes into a cookbook, making it truly a group labor of love from this kitchen and our table to yours.

Before coming to the Spiral House and inspiring this book, Diane studied at the Culinary Institute of America and other cooking schools, operated her own catering business, and was the chef at various restaurants and spiritual retreats. Having cooked professionally to satisfy a wide range of personal tastes, Hagedorn brings an exacting standard to the vegan dishes she prepares at the Spiral House. And although most in the group are vegans, some are not, so we have inevitably created a completely plant-based cookbook that is well-suited to a broad spectrum of the public: vegans, vegetarians, and meat-eaters who are seeking to add more plant-based food to their diet. Many in the group are also gluten-free, and so most of the dishes in our book are gluten-free as well.

Turn the pages and you'll find recipes based on newly popular ingredients like microgreens and quinoa alongside traditional holiday dishes, the kinds of comfort foods from childhood that some of the vegans among us had assumed were a thing of the past, and a variety of scrumptious and inventive dishes.

In these fast-paced and chaotic times, a growing number of people are becoming aware of the importance of social bonds, seeking a way around the isolation they feel. We believe that respect, care, and love of all living things and an awareness of our interconnectedness provide a good antidote.

Not surprisingly, our lunch table is often filled with friends. And this feels just right. But our table is not large enough to accommodate everyone no matter how hard we try . . . and we do try.

For Goodness Sake enables us to share a sense of our loving community and its appreciation for a wholesome and compassionate lifestyle with others beyond our circle. We hope you will enjoy these recipes in good health and at a table where you, too, are surrounded by the warmth of family and friends.

— Patty Livingston and Tom Gottsleben
and the crew at the Spiral House
Saugerties, New York, October 2015

Why Plant-Based?

At the Spiral House, eating well means sharing with others organic, plant-based meals that are nourishing, delicious, and, whenever possible, locally grown. Many of us also regard a plant-based diet as one of the most effective personal choices we can make on behalf of the planet and the life that it supports.

So when does a plant-based diet become vegan? Strictly speaking, a vegan is a person who does not eat or use any animal products, but there are nuances about which vegans can differ markedly. Most wear no leather or animal products; some will. Similarly, there are different views about the use of silk (which is produced by silkworms) and honey (a product from bees who may not have been treated humanely). We all have our comfort levels.

It's better for our health

Eating animal fats and proteins has been shown to raise an individual's risk of developing certain cancers, heart disease, diabetes, and obesity. Animal fats can clog arteries with cholesterol and impede blood flow to the organs. Scientists now know that many of us are able to avoid and manage these illnesses through the lifestyle choices we make.

A plant-based diet rich in fruits, vegetables, whole grains, and legumes is totally free of cholesterol and low in fats (especially saturated fats), while supplying the nutrients one needs for good health: protein, fiber, vitamins, and minerals. (Nuts also add protein but are high in calories and so should be eaten in moderation.)

B_{12} is the one vitamin that can pose a nutritional issue, but this is easily remedied. Nutritional yeast — often added to dishes for its nutty flavor — is an excellent source. Fortified breakfast cereals, soymilk, and meat analogues contain reliable amounts as well. Most multivitamins also include B_{12}.

It's better for the planet

The impact of livestock production on our environment and health is staggering. Highly inefficient, animal agriculture requires disproportionate amounts of land, water, fertilizer, fuel, and other resources. It also pollutes our land and waterways.

Huge livestock farms, which can house hundreds of thousands of pigs, chickens, or cows, produce vast amounts of manure, often generating as much waste as a small city. As a direct result, livestock production is responsible for producing more climate change gases than every vehicle on the planet combined. And it is squandering one of the planet's most precious resources: water. Eight percent of global human water use is now devoted to raising animals for food.

About 13 pounds of feed are required to produce one pound of beef. Many environmentalists believe this plant food could be used so much more efficiently to feed humans worldwide, substantially reducing hunger through more careful planning. Eating meat has become one of the most harmful things we can do to the earth.

A vegan diet is kinder

Large factory farms have forced out most of the small farms that once dotted the American landscape, to the point where the scale of today's agribusiness bears no resemblance to farming as we once thought of it. The dairy and meat industries frequently operate without the kind of government oversight the general public assumes is in place, particularly in an era of government budget cuts. Even free-range chickens and pasture-raised cows — which are surely a minority of the estimated 16 billion animals consumed in the US each year —are typically slaughtered by cruel and horrific means that involve prolonged pain. It is impossible to separate this process from the food we eat.

Being vegan is simpler than ever

Once you familiarize yourself with some new products and substitution methods, it will seem as if you have been preparing plant-based meals forever. Actually, lots of the dishes we've been eating all our lives have been vegan without our giving it a thought: many soups, salads, grain dishes like kasha and bowties, vegetable entrées of all kinds, sauces such as marinara, guacamole, sorbets, and even some of our favorite dark chocolate cakes and fruit pies.

To make it even easier, meat and dairy substitutes are now readily available in supermarkets and health food stores as a direct result of the increasing demand for plant-based foods. (We've listed some of our favorite products and resources at the end of this book, but new items are reaching the market every day so consider our suggestions just a starting point.) Chef Diane has devised so many easy and inventive twists that they will change the way you think about what you buy and how you prepare it to make dishes you will love.

For Goodness Sake was created to appeal to anyone who wants to enjoy delicious plant-based food. Our hope is that the book, along with our companion blog and website (see page 276 about 4goodness-sake.com), will enable all of us to become healthier and better informed, and to walk more gently upon the earth.

For Why Plant-Based sources, see page 276

Starters

Strange Attractor
Sculpture by Tom Gottsleben,
crystal glass, bluestone,
and stainless steel

Feta & Ricotta Cheeses

...mething different. A staple of our vegan kitchen, both "cheeses" use the ...ooked mixture is our house ricotta; the baked mixture is our feta, which ...r. Either version can be added to other dishes for a satisfyingly cheesy ... these can be frozen (see notes), we usually make a double batch.

Makes one 6-inch round

Prepare in advance

1 cup whole almonds, soaked in cold water for 24 hours

Ingredients

1 cup whole almonds

¼ cup fresh-squeezed lemon juice

3 tablespoons plus ¼ cup olive oil

2 cloves garlic, peeled

1¼ teaspoons salt

¼ cup cold water

leaves of 2 sprigs fresh thyme

leaves of 2 sprigs fresh rosemary

Method for ricotta

1. Place the almonds in a bowl and add enough cold water to cover. Let soak for 24 hours. Drain the soaking liquid, rinse the almonds under cold running water, and drain again.

2. Remove the almond skins by squeezing each almond through your fingertips

3. Put peeled almonds in a food processor along with the lemon juice, 3 tablespoons oil, garlic, salt, and cold water. Purée for 10 to 12 minutes, or until very smooth and creamy. The ricotta is ready to use, freeze, or bake to make feta; recipe follows.

Method for feta

1. Follow the three steps for preparing ricotta.

2. Preheat oven to 225 degrees. Line a baking sheet with parchment paper. Dampen your hands with cold water, then flatten cheese to form a 6-inch round about ¾-inch thick. Drizzle ¼ cup oil on top, and sprinkle with thyme and rosemary leaves.

3. Bake for 40 minutes or until the top is slightly firm.

4. Let cool, then wrap and chill in the refrigerator.

Note

• It's important to use fresh-squeezed lemon juice here; it adds a brightness of flavor that you just can't get from bottled lemon juice.

• Cheese can be made up to two days in advance. Keep refrigerated.

• Freezes well; make a double batch.

• You can freeze the baked rounds or the uncooked mixture; but do not bake after freezing.

Buffalo Cauliflower and Tempeh

Serve these spicy bites, separately or together, with your favorite dip or dressing — we use a plant-based ranch. They also give a flavorful kick atop a green salad.

Serves 6 to 8 if making both dishes

For the cauliflower rub

¼ cup light brown sugar

¼ cup paprika

3 tablespoons freshly ground pepper

3 tablespoons salt

1 tablespoon onion powder

1 teaspoon celery seed

½ teaspoon cayenne pepper

1 teaspoon ground cumin

For the cauliflower

1 head cauliflower, cut into florets

2 tablespoons grapeseed oil

¾ cup Frank's Red Hot sauce, or to taste

4 tablespoons melted Earth Balance Vegan Buttery Stick, or to taste

For the tempeh

8 ounces flax or wild rice tempeh

2 tablespoons grapeseed oil

2 tablespoons Earth Balance Vegan Buttery Stick

5 cloves garlic, minced

½ cup vegetable broth

½ cup Frank's Red Hot sauce

2 teaspoons Italian seasoning

celery sticks, for serving

Method for cauliflower

1. Preheat the oven to 400 degrees.

2. Mix the rub ingredients together in a bowl.

3. In another bowl, mix the cauliflower florets with the grapeseed oil, then toss with the rub.

4. Place florets on a parchment-lined cookie sheet and roast until golden brown, about 20 minutes.

5. While the cauliflower roasts, mix Frank's Red Hot sauce with the melted Earth Balance.

6. Toss the warm cauliflower florets with the buttery hot sauce mixture.

Method for tempeh

1. Pull apart or cut the tempeh into small pieces.

2. In a sauté pan large enough to submerge the tempeh in water, add water to cover and bring to a boil. Reduce the heat and simmer until most of the water is absorbed and evaporated, 10 to 15 minutes.

3. Drain any remaining water and return pan with tempeh to the stovetop. Add grapeseed oil and sauté the tempeh until lightly browned. Add the Earth Balance to a corner of the pan. When melted, quickly sauté the garlic. Stir garlic into the tempeh and continue cooking until the tempeh is golden brown but the garlic is not burnt.

4. Add the broth, hot sauce, and Italian seasoning to the pan. Turn the heat to high until the liquid comes to a boil, then reduce heat to a simmer and cook until the liquid is reduced by half.

5. Serve with celery sticks.

Filo Reubens

Surprise family and friends by turning the classic deli sandwich into a flavor-filled vegan finger food. For best results, use a good fresh sauerkraut from the refrigeration section of your market.

Makes 24 triangles

Prepare in advance

Russian Dressing, page 227

Oven-Dried Tomatoes, page 243

Ingredients

half of a 16-ounce box of 9- x 14-inch filo dough, defrosted (see notes)

1 Earth Balance Vegan Buttery Stick, melted

4 ounces vegan cheese slices, cut into small squares

30 oven-dried cherry tomatoes

1½ avocados, pitted and cut in small pieces

2 cups sauerkraut, drained, rinsed, and mixed with ½ cup Russian Dressing

Note
• The night before you plan to make this, put the box of filo in the refrigerator to defrost.
• A tip for beginners: Wider strips (such as the size indicated in this recipe) are easier to work with than narrow strips. If you feel timid about working with filo, you can find good how-to videos online.
• If you want a bite-size appetizer, cut each double sheet into 4 strips. Folding them will require a bit more dexterity.
• These can be made ahead and frozen after completing step 4, then defrosted and baked.
• If you don't use the entire box of filo, you can refreeze the unused sheets. Plan to use the refrozen filo within ten days, or it will be brittle and crack. Try our Spanakopycat (page 154).

Method

1. Preheat the oven to 350 degrees.

2. Gently unfold the defrosted filo dough. Lay one sheet on parchment paper and brush it lightly with melted Earth Balance. Lay a second filo sheet on top of the first and brush it lightly with Earth Balance.

3. Cut the layered filo down the long side into 3-inch-wide strips. This will give you 3 strips from each pair of filo sheets.

4. Place a small amount of cheese, tomatoes, avocado, and sauerkraut mixture at the bottom of each strip (nearest you). Pretend you are folding a flag. Starting with the right corner, fold the dough up towards left edge of the dough to make a triangle. Then fold the stuffed dough to the opposite edge, and continue folding to opposite edge until you reach the end of the filo strip. You should have a triangle-shaped stuffed filo.

5. As you finish filling and folding each piece, place it on a baking sheet lined with parchment paper. Then cover with another sheet of parchment paper and a damp cloth. Covering in this way will keep the completed pieces from drying out while you stuff and fold the rest.

6. Repeat steps 2–5 seven times. You will need a total of 16 filo sheets to get 24 triangles. If you've never worked with filo before you might have some false starts and use more sheets. If you're comfortable working with the dough, you might make a double recipe to use the whole box, and freeze some. (See notes about freezing.)

7. When you finish making all the triangles, remove the cloth and top sheet of parchment paper. Bake until lightly browned, approximately 20 minutes.

d Cheese Bites

comfort food served as bite-size treats. The ingredients and preparation ...milar to our Quintessential Mac and Cheese entrée (page 138), but take a delightfully different turn, leaving you with little tastes of home.

Makes 24 bite-size pieces

Prepare in advance

Savory Cashew Cream Sauce, page 221

Nutty Parm, page 241 (optional)

Ingredients

1 pound quinoa shells or pasta of your choice

1 head cauliflower, cut into chunks

2 tablespoons Earth Balance Vegan Buttery Stick

1 medium onion, finely chopped

3 cloves garlic, finely chopped

2 cups Savory Cashew Cream Sauce

7 ounces Jack-style dairy-free cheese, cubed

7 ounces spicy dairy-free cheese, cubed

1¼ to 2 cups soy creamer

2 tablespoons chopped flat-leaf parsley

2 tablespoons chopped fresh dill

2 pinches of ground nutmeg

salt and freshly ground pepper

cooking spray

Nutty Parm, panko rice bread crumbs, or a combination, for topping.

Method

1. Cook pasta until al dente. Drain, then pulse in food processor to coarsely chop. Transfer to a large bowl.

2. Blanch the cauliflower. Drain, then pulse in food processor to coarsely chop. Add to the chopped pasta.

3. Preheat the oven to 350 degrees.

4. Melt the Earth Balance in a large sauté pan. Sauté the onions and garlic until soft. Add cashew cream and cubed cheeses and stir. Continue cooking on low heat until everything is well combined.

5. Slowly add soy creamer, stirring with a wooden spoon, until the cheese is melted and you have a creamy sauce. It should stick to the back of a wooden spoon, but not be so thick that you can't pour it. You might not need to add all of the soy creamer to get this consistency.

6. Add the cheese sauce, chopped parsley, dill, and nutmeg to the cauliflower-noodle mixture. Taste for salt and season with pepper. If mixture seems too thick, add more soy creamer.

7. Spray the cups of a mini-muffin tin with cooking oil. Fill muffin cups three-quarters full with the mac and cheese mixture. Top with Nutty Parm and/or panko rice bread crumbs and .

8. Bake for 30 minutes until cooked through and lightly golden on top.

Note
• Can make ahead.
• Can refrigerate cooked or uncooked for 2 to 3 days.
• Freezes well cooked or uncooked.

Mediterranean Terrine

The blend of Mediterranean flavors, including our homemade feta "cheese," makes this as memorably delicious as it is colorful and elegant. It takes a bit of time to prepare, but it can be made in advance, which helps with menu-planning for a party table or special meal. You can make one large terrine; or make two small terrines and freeze one of them.

Makes two terrines measuring 8- x 4 ¼- x 2 ½-inches

Prepare in advance

Artisanal Feta Cheese, page 18

Oven-Dried Tomatoes, page 243

Roasted Red Peppers, page 242

Ingredients

4 medium-size beets

2 eggplants, peeled and sliced lengthwise, ½-inch thick

granulated garlic

salt and freshly ground pepper

2 tablespoons olive oil, plus more for grilling eggplant

2 cloves garlic, chopped

1 pound fresh spinach, tough stems trimmed

7 to 8 large unblemished Swiss chard leaves

1 bunch fresh basil leaves

1 pint oven-dried tomatoes

¾ cup Artisanal Feta Cheese

4 roasted red peppers, sliced

Note
• We roast our own peppers and oven-dry our garden tomatoes, but jarred peppers and store-bought dried tomatoes will still make a beautiful terrine.
• Freezes well.
• Patty likes to warm slices of the terrine to serve as a dinner entrée.

Method

1. Boil the beets until tender. Cool, peel, and cut in ½-inch thick slices.

2. Season the eggplant with granulated garlic, salt, and pepper. Drizzle with olive oil and grill on a stovetop grill pan or outdoor grill until browned.

3. Sauté the garlic in 2 tablespoons olive oil, add the spinach, and cook until soft. Dry the spinach on paper towels to remove excess moisture, then chop.

4. Blanch the Swiss chard until just wilted. Drain and add to an ice-water bath. Drain again, pat dry, and remove tough stems.

5. Line a terrine with plastic wrap, allowing extra plastic to extend over the sides of the terrine. Arrange the Swiss chard along the bottom and sides of the terrine, allowing the leaves to hang over the plastic wrap. Layer the ingredients — eggplant, beets, spinach, tomato, whole basil leaves, feta, red pepper — until the layers reach the top of the terrine.

6. When the terrine is full, fold the Swiss chard leaves over the top of the other ingredients, covering them completely. Fold the plastic wrap over the Swiss chard.

7. Place weights across the entire top of the terrine (canned beans work well) and refrigerate overnight. To serve, remove the weights, open the plastic wrap, and flip the terrine upside down to release the contents onto a serving plate.

8. Remove plastic and slice to serve.

Loaded Mushrooms

One side of these mushrooms won't make you taller and the other side won't make you shorter, as happened to Alice during one of her adventures in Wonderland. Here, however, eating the entire mushroom will make you very happy, and eating several will make you quite euphoric.

Serves 12 to 20

Prepare in advance

Basil Pesto, page 232

Nutty Parm, page 241

Ingredients

4 tablespoons olive oil

3 cups packed chopped spinach

24 white mushrooms, all of similar size, stems removed and chopped for stuffing

1 cup finely chopped onion

2 cloves garlic, finely chopped

1½ cups basil pesto

salt and freshly ground pepper to taste

bread crumbs of your choice (we like panko, and rice panko for gluten-free)

4 to 5 heaping tablespoons Nutty Parm

Method

1. Preheat the oven to 350 degrees.

2. Heat 1 tablespoon of olive oil over medium heat and sauté spinach until wilted. Transfer to paper towels, pat dry of any excess moisture, and chop.

3. Clean the mushroom caps. Use a small knife to carefully pry out every little bit of the stem so you'll have a nice clean cavity for stuffing.

4. Heat the remaining 3 tablespoons of olive oil in a large skillet. Sauté the onions, garlic, and chopped mushroom stems until soft.

5. Add the pesto and sautéed spinach to the skillet and season with salt and pepper to taste.

6. Mix in just enough bread crumbs to pull all the stuffing ingredients together. Adjust seasonings to taste. Remove pan from the heat.

7. Fill the mushroom caps with stuffing. Sprinkle each one with Nutty Parm.

8. Line a baking sheet with parchment paper and place the mushrooms on it. If any of the mushrooms won't stay upright, carefully cut a small slice from the bottom so they sit flat.

9. Bake for 25 to 30 minutes.

Note
• Drying the spinach in step 2 is very important or your mushrooms will be soggy.

Eggplant and Beet Napoleon

These little stacks make a colorful starter for a special meal or festive occasion. They're light, tasty, and memorable.

Makes approximately 12 stacks

Prepare in advance

4 medium-size beets, washed, boiled, peeled, and sliced

Artisanal Feta Cheese, page 18

3 Roasted Red Peppers, page 242, sliced in strips

Ingredients

3 long, narrow eggplants, peeled, trimmed, and sliced into 1-inch thick rounds

granulated garlic

salt and freshly ground pepper to taste

olive oil, for drizzling

4 medium-size beets

12 basil leaves

3 medium-size fresh tomatoes, cut into 12 slices

12 slices Artisanal Feta Cheese

3 roasted red peppers

parsley for garnish (optional)

Method

1. Season eggplant rounds with granulated garlic, salt, and pepper. Drizzle slices with olive oil and grill on a grill pan or outdoor grill until browned.

2. Drizzle the beet slices with olive oil and grill on a grill pan or outdoor grill until tender.

3. Top each beet slice with an eggplant round, a basil leaf, a slice of fresh tomato, a slice of feta cheese, and a strip of roasted red pepper.

4. Garnish with parsley, if you like.

Note
• We roast our own peppers, but using jarred peppers is also fine.
• For the best flavor, you really do want to grill the vegetables for this dish, either on an outdoor grill or a stovetop grill pan.

Stuffed Grape Leaves

We'll admit that for mere kitchen mortals, these are a labor of love to make from scratch, especially with freshly harvested grape leaves. But what a delicious way to bring the magic of a Persian garden or the ambience of an Aegean isle to those you love. We like to serve these with the traditional accompaniments shown: hummus, olives, and our homemade feta (page 18).

Makes approximately 40

Ingredients

50 fresh grape leaves
or
1 jar (16 ounces) brined grape leaves, rinsed

3 large onions, finely chopped

5 cloves garlic, chopped

1 cup olive oil

1 cup pine nuts, toasted

1½ cups uncooked short-grain rice

1 cup chopped flat-leaf parsley

½ cup chopped fresh dill

½ cup chopped fresh mint

juice of 2 lemons

1 lemon, sliced

salt and freshly ground pepper to taste

cooking spray

Method

1. If using fresh grape leaves, blanch them briefly in boiling water, then plunge them into an ice-water water bath. Drain and pat dry.

2. Sauté the onions and garlic in olive oil until soft.

3. In a large bowl, combine the onions, garlic, toasted pine nuts, rice, parsley, dill, mint, lemon juice, salt, and pepper.

4. Oil the bottom of a large, heavy pot with cooking spray. Then cover the bottom of the pot with a layer of unstuffed grape leaves.

5. On a flat surface, lay out the grape leaves with the stems toward you and the underside of the leaves facing up (veins are raised on the underside). Trim off the bottom of each stem.

6. Place a tablespoon of the mixture from step 3 in the center of each leaf. Fold one side over the filling, then the other side, then roll up the leaf from the bottom toward the top. Repeat.

7. Arrange the rolled leaves, seam side down, in the pot in layers. Pack the stuffed leaves tightly to help keep them from floating and unrolling while they cook. (Demos are available online.)

8. Pour ½ cup olive oil over grape leaves. Place lemon slices on top. Choose a plate slightly smaller than the circumference of the pot to cover the leaves and keep them submerged; then add enough water to cover by approximately an inch.

9. Bring to a boil, then reduce the heat and cover the pot, keeping the plate in place.

10. Simmer for approximately an hour or until the rice is cooked and leaves are tender.

Pesto-Stuffed Cherry Tomatoes

A visually stunning presentation and a mouth-watering taste.

Makes 50 to 60

Prepare in advance

Basil Pesto, page 232

Ingredients

4 tablespoons basil pesto

8 ounces non-dairy cream cheese

2 pints large cherry tomatoes

Method

1. Mix the pesto and cream cheese in a bowl until well combined.

2. Rinse the tomatoes and pat dry.

3. Using a serrated knife, carefully cut off a thin sliver from the bottom of each tomato, just enough so it will sit flat.

4. Slice off the top of each tomato and scoop out the seeds and pulp.

5. Fill a pastry bag with the cream cheese mixture (or fill a zip-tight plastic bag, then snip off a corner). Squeeze filling into each tomato cavity.

Beet "Tartare"

Roasted beets, minced and marinated — we think this is just about the fullest expression of a beet there is. A little goes a long way; you may find yourself eating some of this ruby-red tartare before dinner one night and as the accompaniment to your main meal the next.

Serves 4

Prepare in advance

Artisanal Feta Cheese, page 18

For the beets

4 medium-size beets

olive oil

Artisanal Feta Cheese, for garnish

chopped chives, for garnish

For the dressing

4 tablespoons olive oil

2 shallots, thinly sliced

juice of ½ orange

2 teaspoons Bragg Liquid Aminos

2 teaspoons capers

salt and freshly ground pepper to taste

Method

1. Preheat the oven to 350 to 375 degrees.

2. Wash and dry beets well, then rub them with oil.

3. Roast the beets for 45 minutes to 1 hour, until fork-tender. When cool enough to handle, peel.

4. While the beets roast, mix the dressing ingredients.

5. Chop the beets into a small dice.

6. Pour the dressing over the diced beets and let them marinate for 20 to 30 minutes.

7. Place a ring mold (3½- x 2-inches) on a serving plate. Scoop the marinated beets into the mold, pressing firmly. To serve, slowly lift the mold straight up, away from the beets. Top with crumbled Artisanal Feta Cheese and chopped chives. Repeat to shape 3 more portions.

Note
• The marinated beets can also be scooped and served in a lettuce cup.

Guacamole

The Aztecs started it, the Mexicans picked up the ball, and we Americans can recognize a very good thing. Here, the Spiral House kitchen crew adds its own tribute to this tradition.

Serves 8 to 10

Ingredients

8 avocados, peeled, pitted, and cubed

8 small plum tomatoes, chopped

5 cloves garlic, finely chopped

1 medium-size red onion, finely chopped

1 small jalapeño pepper, seeded and finely chopped

2 tablespoons chopped fresh cilantro

1 teaspoon ground cumin

salt and freshly ground pepper to taste

juice of 2 limes

Method

Mix everything together and serve.

Krispy Kale

The key to crispy kale chips that everyone will love? Thoroughly dry the washed leaves before tossing with oil. And keep checking the kale as it bakes: undercooked kale will be soggy; over-cooked chips will taste burned.

Ingredients

1 pound kale, stems and large ribs removed

¼ cup olive oil

1 clove garlic, minced

salt and freshly ground pepper

Method

1. Preheat the oven to 375 degrees.

2. In a large bowl, toss the kale with the olive oil and garlic.

3. Spread the kale leaves in a single layer on two baking sheets and roast for approximately 15 minutes, rotating the pans 180 degrees in the oven halfway through. Leaves will shrink to chip size.

4. When kale is crisp, remove from the oven and season with salt and pepper.

Note
• For a change of flavor, dust kale with chili powder or dried oregano in step 2.

Spinach Dip with Chipotle and Lime

With this highly flavored creamy dip, your crudité will quickly disappear, so be sure to prepare a lot of extra veggies.

Makes 3 cups

Ingredients

8 ounces vegan cream cheese, softened

½ cup Just Mayo

½ cup vegan sour cream

½ cup sliced scallions

6 cloves garlic, chopped

⅓ cup chopped fresh cilantro

1 tablespoon chopped chipotle peppers in adobo

1½ tablespoons honey

2 tablespoons fresh-squeezed lime juice

¾ teaspoon salt

freshly ground pepper to taste

2 (10-ounce) packages frozen chopped spinach, thawed and well drained but not cooked

Method

1. Add all the ingredients except the spinach to the bowl of a food processor. Pulse until smooth.

2. Wrap the spinach in a clean kitchen towel and twist it to wring out all the moisture. Then add the spinach to the food processor with the other ingredients and pulse until just combined.

Walnut-Vegetable Balls

We think these are the best "meatballs" ever. Just make sure the herbs are fresh and don't skimp on the garlic. Serve them as an appetizer or with your favorite marinara sauce over pasta.

Makes 24 large meatballs

Prepare in advance

Nutty Parm, page 241

1 cup mashed potatoes

Ingredients

2 onions, chopped

5 cloves garlic, chopped

olive oil, for sautéing

2 small eggplants, peeled and cubed

2 pounds spinach, tough stems trimmed

4 cups walnuts

1 pound cremini mushrooms, sliced

1 cup Nutty Parm

1 tablespoon fennel seeds

½ teaspoon chopped fresh thyme

1 tablespoon Italian seasoning

4 large leaves basil, rolled and cut crosswise into ribbons

½ cup chopped flat-leaf parsley

2 large russet potatoes, mashed to make approximately 1 cup

4 flax eggs (1 flax egg = 1 tablespoon flaxseed soaked in 3 tablespoons warm water for 5 minutes)

Method

1. Preheat the oven to 350 degrees.

2. Sauté the onions and garlic in olive oil. Add the eggplant and mushrooms and cook until soft. Remove from pan to make way for the spinach.

3. Sauté the spinach in more olive oil. Dry on a paper towel-lined baking sheet and blot with another paper towel. Then roughly chop the spinach.

4. Meanwhile, on another baking sheet, toast walnuts in a 350-degree oven. Keep an eye on them, shaking the pan occasionally to prevent burning.

5. In a food processor, pulse the eggplant mixture, spinach, toasted walnuts, mashed potatoes, and flax eggs until the texture is soft but not mushy. Move the mixture to a large bowl.

6. Add the Nutty Parm, fennel seeds, thyme, Italian seasoning, basil, and parsley. Stir to combine.

7. Cover the bowl with plastic wrap and let mixture rest in the refrigerator for 6 to 8 hours or overnight.

8. Line a baking sheet with parchment paper and lightly oil the paper. Using a tablespoon, shape the walnut mixture into balls and bake in a 350-degree oven for 30 minutes.

Note
• You'll need to plan ahead on this recipe as the walnut mixture should be refrigerated for 6 to 8 hours before shaping into rounds and baking.
• Can freeze cooked or uncooked.

Walnut-Vegetable Balls in the foreground, on a party table with most of the other appetizers in this section.

Soups

Rainbow Knots
on the terraced walls of the Spiral House.
Sculpture by Tom Gottsleben,
crystal glass, bluestone, and stainless steel

Beyond Miso Soup

A staple of Japanese cuisine, eaten with any meal of the day including breakfast, miso soup is made of a stock (called a *dashi*) into which miso paste is stirred. The soup can be light or hearty, depending on the type of miso used, and typically includes two or more types of seaweed, a few vegetables, and perhaps some tofu for protein. Chef Diane's elegant version is one to linger over as you savor the complex flavors of the broth, the earthy taste of the mushrooms, and the crispy freshness of the snow peas.

Serves 4 to 6

Ingredients

3 quarts vegetable stock or water

1 piece dried wakame seaweed

1 ounce dried wild shiitake mushrooms

1 large stalk lemongrass, bruised (see note)

1 onion, cut in half

2 cloves garlic, peeled

1 strip kelp seaweed

1 cup sliced fresh shiitake mushroom caps

1 heaping tablespoon brown rice or red miso, or to taste

soft tofu, cubed (optional)

finely chopped scallions, for garnish

snow peas, strings removed, finely chopped, for garnish

Method

1. In a large pot, combine the stock or water, wakame, dried mushrooms, lemongrass, onion, garlic, and kelp. Bring to a boil. Reduce the heat and simmer, uncovered, for 1 hour.

2. Strain through a colander, reserving the stock and, if desired, the dried mushrooms. Return the stock to the pot.

3. Add the fresh mushrooms and continue to simmer for another 15 minutes. Optional: Slice the dried shiitakes used in the stock and return them to the soup along with the fresh mushrooms.

4. Just before serving, add miso to a small amount of stock and stir to blend into a paste, then return the mixture to the soup. Add the tofu, if desired. Do not let the soup boil after adding the miso, as boiling destroys some of miso's nutritional value.

5. Serve immediately, garnished with scallions and snow peas.

Note
• For a gluten-free soup: Miso may include fermented wheat or barley, so check the label.
• Using a vegetable stock instead of water is part of what makes Diane's version so deeply satisfying, warranting the status of "beyond" in the recipe's title.
• The easiest way to get the unique flavor and aroma of lemongrass without fussing with its fibrous texture: Cut off each end of the stalk, remove the tough outer leaves, and bruise the remaining stalk with the flat side of a knife or cleaver. Add to soup and remove before serving.

Springtime Asparagus Soup

When asparagus are plentiful — in your own garden or at the farmer's market — seize the moment to make soup that smells and tastes like spring.

Serves 6

Prepare in advance

2½ quarts Roasted Vegetable Stock, page 246

Ingredients

4 pounds asparagus

2½ quarts vegetable stock

4 medium-size Yukon gold potatoes, peeled and cubed

4 tablespoons Earth Balance Vegan Buttery Stick

2 leeks, roots removed, dark woody outer leaves discarded, whites and tender green portion chopped and rinsed well

3 tablespoons finely chopped garlic

salt and freshly ground pepper to taste

3 tablespoons chopped fresh dill

Method

1. To prepare the asparagus: Cut off the tips to use for garnish; cut off the tough ends to enhance the stock; coarsely chop the centers.

2. In a large soup pot, heat the vegetable stock, add the asparagus ends and cubed potatoes, and cook until soft. Remove and discard the asparagus ends.

3. While the stock is cooking, melt the Earth Balance in a large pan. Add the chopped asparagus and leeks and sauté for a few minutes. Add the garlic, season with salt and pepper, and continue cooking until the vegetables are soft. Mix in 2 tablespoons of dill.

4. Add the sautéed vegetables to the stock. Simmer for 15 to 20 minutes.

5. In a food processor or with an immersion blender, purée the soup. (Tip: To control consistency in puréed soups, set aside some of the stock and add it to the purée as needed.)

6. Very briefly blanch the asparagus tips until just tender. Drain and reserve until ready to serve.

Garnish the soup with asparagus tips and the remaining tablespoon of dill.

Watermelon Gazpacho

The bright flavors of watermelon, mint, and lime add a winning twist to traditional gazpacho. This combination was unheard of a decade ago, and now we (and apparently many others) can't get enough of it.

Serves 12

Ingredients

5 pounds ripe tomatoes, stemmed and cut into chunks

1 cup roughly chopped celery

1 red bell pepper, stemmed, seeded, and roughly chopped

3 cucumbers, peeled, seeded, and roughly chopped

5 large shallots, chopped

5 cups seeded and cubed watermelon

3 slices white bread, toasted and cubed

6 tablespoons sherry wine vinegar

3 tablespoons extra-virgin olive oil

5 tablespoons chopped fresh herbs (a combination of basil, mint, parsley)

1½ teaspoons salt

½ teaspoon ground white pepper

juice of 1 lime

optional garnishes:

1 ripe avocado, peeled, pitted, and sliced

lime slices

Note
• Can refrigerate for up to 3 days.

Method

1. Working in batches, purée the vegetables, watermelon, and bread cubes in a blender or food processor.

2. Stir in vinegar, oil, herbs, salt, pepper, and lime.

3. Refrigerate at least 6 hours or overnight.

Mom's Gazpacho

This recipe goes back at least 50 years, long before there was even the glimmer of a Spiral House. Patty's mom, Joan Tweedy, found it in a recipe booklet that had been put together by members of her needlepoint group in Connecticut. After all these years, it's still one of Patty's favorites.

Serves 6 to 8

Ingredients

3 large tomatoes, finely chopped

2 large cucumbers, peeled, seeded, finely chopped

1 medium onion, finely chopped

2 large cloves garlic, finely chopped

1 green pepper, seeded and finely chopped

1 shallot, finely chopped

4 stalks celery, cubed

½ of a 4-ounce jar of pimientos

1 to 1½ quarts Knudsen's Very Veggie Spicy Juice (or your favorite tomato juice)

¼ cup olive oil

⅓ cup good red wine vinegar

½ teaspoon Sriracha-style hot sauce

¼ cup chopped fresh basil

½ cup chopped flat-leaf parsley

juice of ½ lemon

1½ teaspoons salt

freshly ground pepper to taste

Method

1. Purée half of the chopped vegetables in a food processor.

2. Combine the rest of the chopped vegetables, the tomato juice, herbs, and seasonings. Stir in the puréed vegetables.

3. Refrigerate at least 6 hours or overnight.

Chilled Cucumber Dill Soup

On a hot day, we are always delighted to have this perfect summer soup for lunch. The mild taste of the cucumber is offset by the boldness of the dill. It's refreshingly delicious, quick, and requires no cooking at all.

Serves 8 to 10

Ingredients

1 cup vegan sour cream

8 cucumbers, peeled, seeded and chopped

½ cup roughly chopped fresh dill

2 cups finely chopped chives

1 tablespoon salt

1 teaspoon ground white pepper

1 tablespoon Bragg Liquid Aminos

3 teaspoons prepared horseradish

1 teaspoon Worcestershire sauce

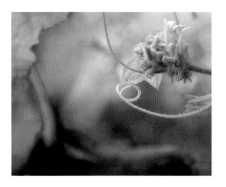

Method

1. Set aside ½ cup of the chives, then combine all the remaining ingredients in a blender or food processor. Process until smooth.

2. Served chilled. Garnish with the reserved chives and a sprig of dill.

Note
• Can refrigerate for 2 to 3 days.

led Corn Chowder

Who doesn't love a good corn chowder? It lands near the top of any list of comfort foods. Chef Diane grills the corn first and then adds both the kernels and the cobs to the chowder to cook, removing the cobs only near the end. Except for a bit of peeling, chopping, and cubing, this recipe is super simple for a soup that has such a smoky kick and depth of flavor.

Serves 8 to 10

Prepare in advance

1½ quarts Roasted Vegetable Stock, page 246

Ingredients

6 ears of corn

2 tablespoons grapeseed oil

2 large onions or leeks, chopped

5 stalks celery, chopped

4 medium-size Yukon gold potatoes, peeled and cubed

1 red bell pepper, seeded and chopped

3 large cloves garlic, chopped

¼ teaspoon cayenne pepper

1½ tablespoons Bragg Liquid Aminos

1½ quarts vegetable stock

1 tablespoon chopped fresh thyme

salt and freshly ground pepper to taste

hot sauce (optional)

¼ cup chopped flat-leaf parsley

Method

1. Grill the corn and remove the kernels. Reserve both cobs and kernels.

2. Heat the oil in a large pot, then add the onions, celery, potatoes, red pepper, garlic, cayenne, and the Bragg and cook until the vegetables begin to soften, around 5 minutes.

3. Add the stock, corn kernels, cobs, and thyme. Simmer over medium heat for 30 minutes.

4. Remove the cobs. Purée half of the mixture in a food processor.

5. Return the purée to the pot and simmer the chowder 10 minutes more.

6. Taste for salt and pepper. Add hot sauce to taste, if desired.

7. Garnish with parsley.

Note
• Grilling the corn on an outdoor grill gives the best flavor, but a stovetop grill pan works well, too.
• Refrigerates well.
• Freezes well.

30-Minute Broccoli Soup

With broccoli available year-round, this easy and budget-friendly soup is a staple at the Spiral House. You can add some more muscle with an extra dash of Bragg Liquid Aminos or give it a creamy touch with a swirl of vegan sour cream. Start a supper with this soup or pair it with our Better-than-Chicken Salad (page 111) for a perfect lunch.

Serves 8

Ingredients

3 bunches of broccoli

2 tablespoons olive oil

4 cloves garlic, chopped

1 onion, diced

salt and freshly ground pepper to taste

Bragg Liquid Aminos (optional)

Note
• Can make ahead.
• Refrigerates well.
• Freezes well.
• To add protein, stir in a can of rinsed and drained cannellini beans in step 7.

Method

1. Separate 1 broccoli head into small florets and set aside for garnish.

2. Discard the tough ends of the broccoli stems. Roughly chop the remaining 2 heads and all the stems.

3. Bring a large pot of salted water to a boil. Blanch the broccoli florets that you will use for garnish for just a few minutes. Use a strainer or other scoop to remove the florets; set them aside.

4. Add the remainder of the chopped broccoli to the pot. Cook until tender.

5. While the broccoli cooks, heat the olive oil in a sauté pan. Add the garlic and onion and sweat until translucent.

6. When tender, drain the broccoli and reserve the cooking water.

7. Combine the cooked garlic, onion, and broccoli in the soup pot with 3 cups of the reserved cooking water and use an immersion blender to purée. Add about 3 cups more of the reserved cooking water, more or less depending on the desired consistency.

   (If you don't have an immersion blender, you can use a food processor or blender for this step.)

8. Season with salt and pepper to taste. Add a dash of Bragg, if desired.

9. Pour the soup into serving bowls. Garnish with blanched broccoli florets.

Tomato Fusion

This one's not a tomato soup, and it's not a borscht, though it boasts ingredients found in both. So we've called it a fusion, its own blend of cultures, vegetables, and seasonings, all existing in perfect harmony, with a flavor and a color that we find truly mesmerizing.

Serves 6

Prepare in advance

1 quart Roasted Vegetable Stock, page 246

Ingredients

3 medium-size beets

1 large leek, roots removed, dark woody outer leaves discarded, whites and tender green portion roughly chopped and rinsed well

4 cloves garlic, chopped

grapeseed oil

1 large onion, chopped

3 stalks celery, chopped

2 bay leaves

2 tablespoons Bragg Liquid Aminos

3 medium-size potatoes, peeled and sliced

1 (14-ounce) can fire-roasted, crushed tomatoes

2 (28-ounce) cans crushed tomatoes or 12 plum tomatoes, peeled

1 quart vegetable stock

2 tablespoons each chopped fresh herbs such as dill, parsley, and basil

salt and freshly ground pepper to taste

Note
• Freezes well.

Method

1. Boil the beets for approximately 45 minutes, or until tender. When they are cool enough to handle, peel them.

2. In a large pot, sauté the leeks and garlic in grapeseed oil.

3. Add the chopped onion, celery, bay leaves, and Bragg and cook until soft.

4. Add the potatoes and tomatoes. Let everything simmer for approximately 10 minutes.

5. Slice the beets and add them to the pot, along with the stock, dill, parsley, basil, salt, and pepper.

6. When the ingredients have softened, purée the soup with an immersion blender or food processor. Top with additional herbs and serve.

Indian-Spiced Red Lentil Soup

As you prepare this soup, the coriander, cumin, turmeric, and red pepper flakes will conjure visions of India, complete with maharajas, brightly-woven saris, and melodic ragas. Lentils cook so much more quickly than other legumes, so you can have this high-protein soup on the table in under an hour.

Serves 8 to 10

Ingredients

1 tablespoon coriander seeds

1 tablespoon cumin seeds

8 cloves garlic, peeled

1 teaspoon salt

3 tablespoons coconut oil

2 large onions, diced

5 stalks celery, chopped

3 carrots, diced

2 tablespoons ground turmeric

¼ teaspoon crushed red pepper flakes

2 bay leaves

3½ cups red lentils, rinsed

2 quarts water, or more as needed

salt and freshly ground pepper to taste

lemon wedges, for serving

Method

1. In a small sauté pan, toast the cumin and coriander seeds on the stovetop for just a few minutes, until fragrant.

2. Using a mortar and pestle, pound the garlic and toasted seeds with the salt into a paste.

3. In a large pot, heat the coconut oil. Add the onions, celery, and carrots and cook for a few minutes until soft. Then add the turmeric, crushed red pepper flakes, and bay leaves.

4. Add the garlic paste to the sautéed vegetables and stir everything together. Cook for a few minutes.

5. Add the rinsed lentils and water to cover. If the soup becomes too thick during cooking, you can add more water later.

6. Cook for approximately 20 minutes or until the lentils are soft and breaking apart. If the soup seems too thick, add more water. Remove bay leaves. Check seasoning, adding black pepper and more salt to taste.

7. Serve with lemon wedges.

Note
• Freezes well.

Southwest Black Bean Soup

This crowd-pleaser is packed with flavor — the smoky, spicy broth filled with the discrete tastes of bean, corn, and tomato. Each spoonful delivers a surprise and leaves you eager for the next.

Serves 6 to 8

Prepare in Advance

4 cups cooked black beans

1½ quarts Roasted Vegetable Stock, page 246

Ingredients

2 tablespoons grapeseed oil

1 large onion, chopped

6 cloves garlic, chopped fine

2 large leeks, roots and tough green leaves discarded, the remainder sliced thin and soaked in water to release dirt

6 stalks celery, chopped

4 carrots, peeled and chopped

½ red bell pepper, chopped

4 cups cooked black beans

1 (28-ounce) can fire-roasted tomatoes

1½ quarts vegetable stock

1 cup fresh or frozen corn

salt and freshly ground pepper to taste

2 teaspoons ground cumin

1 teaspoon smoked paprika

½ teaspoon ancho chili powder

1 teaspoon chipotle chili powder

1 tablespoon chopped cilantro, plus more for garnish

¼ cup chopped parsley, plus more for garnish

dairy-free sour cream, avocado, lime wedges, for garnish (optional)

Method

1. In a large pot, heat the grapeseed oil and then sauté the onion, garlic, leeks, celery, carrots, and red pepper until soft.

2. Add the black beans, tomatoes, stock, and corn to the pot. Season with salt and pepper, then stir in the cumin, paprika, and both chili powders. Bring to a boil, reduce heat to a simmer, then stir in the cilantro and parsley.

3. Simmer for 30 minutes, until all the flavors have melded.

4. Garnish with the extra cilantro and parsley, plus sour cream, avocado, and lime wedges, as desired.

African Peanut Soup with Yams

The seasonings in this rich soup — cilantro, garlic, ginger, cumin, coriander, cinnamon, turmeric, and pepper — comprise much of the backbone of African cuisine. The color, the aroma, and the lively flavors are truly memorable.

Serves 6

Ingredients

2 to 3 tablespoons grapeseed oil

1 large onion, diced

1 small bunch cilantro, stems finely sliced and leaves chopped separately

3 large cloves garlic, finely chopped

1 (1-inch) piece fresh ginger, peeled and finely chopped or grated

1½ teaspoons ground cumin

1 teaspoon ground coriander

½ teaspoon ground cinnamon

½ teaspoon ground turmeric

1 teaspoon red pepper flakes

2 pinches of ground cloves

1 cup crushed canned tomatoes

4 medium-size yams, washed and chopped into 1-inch cubes

1¼ teaspoons salt, or to taste

1½ quarts water

¾ cup chunky organic peanut butter

1 (14-ounce) can unsweetened coconut milk

½ cup salted toasted peanuts, plus more for garnish

juice of 1 small lime, plus wedges for garnish

Method

1. In a large pot, warm the oil on medium-high heat and then add the onion and cilantro stems. Stir and cook until the onions are soft, 5 to 10 minutes.

2. Stir in the garlic, ginger, cumin, coriander, cinnamon, turmeric, red pepper flakes, and cloves.

3. Add the tomatoes, yams, salt, and water. Bring to a boil, lower the heat and simmer, partially covered, until the potatoes are tender, 20 to 30 minutes. Stir in the peanut butter and then the coconut milk.

4. Purée 3 cups of the soup in a blender until creamy and return to the pot. (If you want a smooth soup, purée the entire soup.) Taste for salt, then add half of the chopped cilantro leaves to the pot.

5. Chop the toasted peanuts and mix them with the remaining cilantro leaves.

6. Ladle the soup into bowls. To each bowl, add a few pinches of red pepper flakes, some lime juice, and a spoonful of the peanut-cilantro mixture.

Serve with the remaining toasted peanuts and the lime wedges on the side.

Note
• This soup has so much flavor that you don't need to use homemade stock; water will suffice.

Fennel, Leek, and Potato Soup

Fennel adds a new spin to a favorite comfort food. In this version, the potato and fennel retain their identities in the wonderfully rich broth, rather than being puréed to a uniform consistency.

Serves 6 to 8

Prepare in advance

2½ quarts Roasted Vegetable Stock, page 246

Ingredients

2 fennel bulbs, thinly sliced, fronds chopped and reserved

2 large leeks, roots removed, dark woody outer leaves discarded, whites and tender green portion thinly sliced and rinsed well

2 celery stalks, thinly sliced

4 cloves garlic, chopped

2 tablespoons olive oil

6 to 7 medium-size Yukon gold potatoes, peeled and cubed

salt and freshly ground pepper to taste

2½ quarts vegetable stock

leaves from 3 sprigs of thyme

small bunch flat-leaf parsley, chopped

Method

1. In a large pot, sauté the fennel, leeks, celery, and garlic in olive oil until soft.

2. Add the potatoes, season with salt and pepper, and sauté for 5 minutes more.

3. Add the stock, thyme, and parsley to the pot. Bring to a boil, then reduce the heat and simmer for 45 minutes to an hour, until the potatoes are tender but not falling apart.

4. Garnish with the reserved fennel fronds and serve.

Note

• If you want a cold, vischyssoise-style soup: Purée the soup after step 3 and chill. Before ladling the chilled soup into bowls, stir in your preferred plant-based milk, creamer, or yogurt.

Mighty Minestrone

This hearty soup is no less than a meal in a bowl and invites you to make use of the vegetables, seasonings, and beans that you have on hand. It will warm your soul any time you eat it but on a cold winter day it's downright medicinal.

Serves 6

Prepare in advance

1½ quarts Roasted Vegetable Stock, page 246

Nutty Parm, page 241

Ingredients

1½ cups chopped onion

4 cloves garlic, chopped

3 tablespoons olive oil

6 celery stalks, chopped with greens

4 carrots, chopped

1 zucchini, chopped

1 teaspoon chopped fresh thyme

½ teaspoon dried oregano

½ cup chopped flat-leaf parsley

5 fresh basil leaves, torn in pieces

2 bay leaves

1½ quarts vegetable stock

1 (28-ounce) can diced tomatoes

1 (15-ounce) can cannellini beans, drained

1½ cups ditalini pasta (or shells or any other small pasta)

2 cups fresh chopped spinach

4 tablespoons Nutty Parm

rosemary sprigs or other chopped herbs for garnish (optional)

Method

1. In a soup pot over low heat, sweat the onions and garlic with olive oil for 5 to 6 minutes, until the vegetables are shiny.

2. Add the celery, carrots, zucchini, thyme, oregano, parsley, basil, and bay leaves. Cook for 10 minutes.

3. Add the stock and tomatoes. Cook over low heat for 20 minutes.

4. While the soup is cooking, bring a pot of water to a boil, generously salt it, and when it returns to a boil, cook the pasta until al dente and drain.

5. Add the cannellini beans to the soup pot. Simmer for 10 minutes more.

6. Stir in the cooked pasta and the spinach. When the spinach has wilted, turn off the heat.

7. Garnish each bowl of the soup with Nutty Parm and additional herbs if desired.

Note
• Refrigerates well.
• Freezes well.

...ll of the Wild Rice Soup

nutty flavor of the wild rice and the woodsy taste of the mushrooms are the star ingredients in this satisfying vegetable soup. Everyone wants Diane to make this for them when they're sick. Then again, everyone also wants it when they are well.

Serves 6 to 8

Prepare in advance

2½ quarts Roasted Vegetable Stock, page 246

Ingredients

1 cup wild rice, uncooked

3 cups water

1 teaspoon salt

2 tablespoons grapeseed oil

1 tablespoon Earth Balance Vegan Buttery Stick

2 white onions, diced

4 cloves garlic, finely chopped

1 pound fresh shiitake mushrooms, stems removed and discarded, caps wiped clean and sliced

5 stalks celery, thinly sliced

3 large carrots, diced

2 small fennel bulbs, thinly sliced

2½ quarts vegetable stock, or more as needed

salt and freshly ground pepper to taste

1 ounce dried porcini mushrooms, reconstituted according to package directions, soaking water reserved

3 sprigs thyme

½ cup chopped flat-leaf parsley

1 bay leaf

1 (5-ounce) package whole roasted and peeled chestnuts, halved

Method

1. Thoroughly clean the wild rice by rinsing it three times with three changes of hot tap water.

2. Put the rice in a medium-size pot, cover with water, and bring to a boil. Add 1 teaspoon salt and reduce heat to a simmer. Cover and cook until rice is al dente, approximately 15 minutes. When done, set aside until step 3.

2. In a soup pot, heat the grapeseed oil and Earth Balance. Sauté the onions and garlic until soft. Add the shiitake mushrooms and continue cooking for approximately 5 minutes.

3. Add the celery, carrots, and fennel, stirring well to combine with the other ingredients. Cook for several minutes, then add the stock, salt and pepper, porcini mushrooms with their soaking liquid, the herbs, chestnuts, cooked wild rice, and any remaining water in the rice pot.

4. Simmer the soup for 20 minutes until the rice is tender. Remove and discard the bay leaf and thyme sprigs.

Note
• Cooking times assume that you are using the hand-harvested, grayish-green true wild rice. Jet black rice labeled as "wild" is cultivated for commercial production; it's less flavorful and takes at least twice as long to cook as hand-harvested rice.
• Refrigerates well.
• Freezes well.

Dancing for Rain

One year a summer-long drought was so severe that we found
ourselves giving our plants just enough water to keep them
alive. Inspired by Native American traditions, Anjali Bermain and
Carie Salberg, our "garden angels," offered to do a rain dance.
And dance they did, to the song "Waterfall" by Lucious Trance,
invoking all the earth mothers — Shakti and Durga, Kali and Pele,
Tara and Quan Yin, Mary and White Buffalo. The next day there
was a deluge. Oh how we love the unexplainable.

Salads

Life Seed (foreground) and *Syzygy* (middle ground)
Sculpture by Tom Gottsleben,
polished bluestone and stainless steel

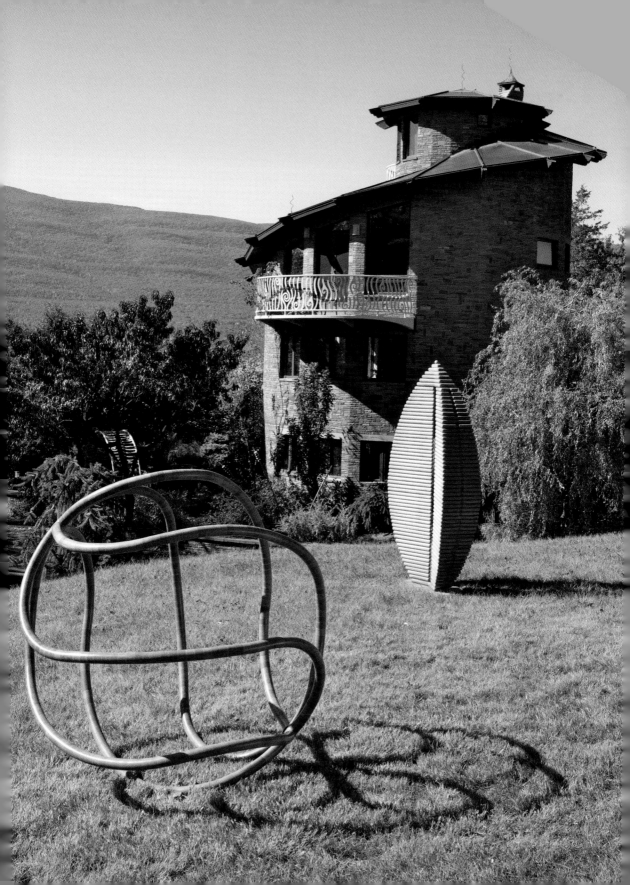

ɪral House Salad with Asian Vinaigrette

What's in a spiral? In mathematics, it can be various kinds of curves in two- or three-dimensional space. In spiritual symbolism, it can represent unity and transformation, the ability to expand outward and contract inward at the same time, never losing connection to the center. And in our Spiral House Salad, it's zucchini, carrots, daikon, cucumbers, celery, and sweet peppers, sliced in a spiralizer with love.

Serves 6

For the salad

2 to 3 cucumbers, peeled

2 large zucchini

3 large carrots

1 daikon radish

3 stalks celery, thinly sliced on
an angle

2 large red and/or green bell peppers,
cut into matchstick strips

For the dressing

Makes ½ cup

Whisk ingredients together. Adjust to
your personal taste.

3 scallions, chopped

3 cloves garlic, chopped

2 tablespoons grated fresh ginger

2 tablespoons brown rice vinegar

2½ tablespoons grapeseed oil

3 tablespoons umeboshi plum vinegar

2 tablespoons mirin

3 tablespoons shoyu soy sauce or
tamari

3 dashes toasted sesame oil

1 tablespoon chopped fresh cilantro

Note
• This is one of those dishes where
your hands are the best tool for tossing the veggies with the dressing.
• Leftover dressing can be stored in
the refrigerator for 3 days.

Method

1. Using a spiral vegetable slicer, "spiralize" the
   cucumbers. Set them in a colander to allow some
   of the liquid to drain.

2. Continue spiral-slicing the zucchini, carrots, and
   daikon, then combine them in a bowl.

3. Add the celery, peppers, and drained cucumbers
   to the bowl.

4. Mix in enough dressing to coat the vegetables and
   enjoy.

Avocado and Citrus Salad with Magical Microgreens

We grow our own microgreens year-round under grow lights because these baby greens of between 10 and 14 days old have been shown to pack many, many times the amount of vitamins and other phytochemicals found in their grown-up relatives. We eat so much of them, in fact, that Tom has his very own hand-thrown bowl for this purpose. See our growing tips on page 276.

Serves 4 to 6

For the salad

1 cup microgreens

1 grapefruit, cut into wedges, membrane removed (see note)

2 blood oranges, cut into wedges, membrane removed (see note)

2 avocados, peeled, pitted, and cubed

1 cup peeled, shredded carrot

½ daikon radish, peeled, thinly sliced

½ cup toasted and chopped walnuts

For the dressing

¼ cup olive oil

¼ cup fresh lemon juice

4 cloves garlic, finely chopped

1 teaspoon maple syrup

¼ cup fresh orange juice

¼ cup fresh grapefruit juice

salt and freshly ground pepper

Note
• To prepare citrus segments: With a sharp knife, cut off top and bottom of fruit, then cut off and discard skin and white pith. Working over a small bowl to catch the juices, cut each segment from its surrounding membranes. Reserve segments in another small bowl.

Method

1. Carefully and lightly wash the microgreens and air dry.

2. In a large bowl, combine the microgreens with all the remaining salad ingredients

3. Whisk the dressing ingredients in a small bowl. Then lightly dress and toss the salad.

Andrea's Sesame-Ginger Kale Salad

The inspiration for this salad came from a vegan cooking class at Woodstock's Garden Cafe on the Green. But being of the more is better school, Andrea added ingredients each time she made it until her quest for "Perfection!" began turning into our cries of "Enough!" That said, it is so delicious that people who ordinarily might not eat kale can happily make a meal of this salad.

Serves 4 to 6 as a salad, 4 as a lunch entrée

Ingredients

1 bunch kale

¼ medium head purple cabbage, white core removed, thinly sliced

3 carrots, peeled and coarsely grated

4 scallions, white and tender green parts, thinly sliced on a diagonal

1 tablespoon grated fresh ginger

3 tablespoons fresh lemon juice

3 tablespoons toasted sesame oil

1½ tablespoons maple syrup

½ teaspoon salt

freshly ground pepper to taste

pinch or two of cayenne pepper

1 (6-ounce) package organic baked tofu, cut into ½-inch cubes (optional)

½ cup peanuts (or cashews), toasted

⅓ cup sesame seeds, toasted

½ cup golden raisins

Method

1. Wash the kale and pat dry. Strip the leaves off the stems.

2. Stack 6 stripped leaves on top of one another and tightly roll them lengthwise like a cigar. Cut crosswise in thin strips. Continue cutting the kale in this way.

3. In a large bowl, toss together the kale, cabbage, carrots, and scallions.

4. Add the ginger, lemon juice, toasted sesame oil, maple syrup, salt and pepper and cayenne to taste. Toss well.

5. Add the tofu, nuts, sesame seeds, and raisins. Toss everything together.

Note
• Refrigerates well for 2 to 4 days.
• You could add up to another tablespoon each of lemon juice and sesame oil, and ½ tablespoon of maple syrup, if desired.

Barley and Kale with Citrus Dressing

A versatile grain with a rich nutty flavor, barley is an excellent source of vitamins, minerals, and fiber. Combining it with kale makes a substantial and earthy salad, while the citrus-herb dressing adds a bright, light note. This is a great dish to make for a crowd, and one that keeps well for a few days. You can easily make half the recipe if you want a smaller amount.

Serves 12

For the salad

2 cups barley, uncooked

5 avocados

5 cups chopped kale (about 2 bunches, stems removed)

6 tomatoes, chopped

1 cup sunflower or sesame seeds, toasted

For the dressing

juice of 2 limes

juice of 1 lemon

juice of 1 orange

4 scallions, white and green parts, chopped

2 tablespoons chopped flat-leaf parsley

¼ cup chopped fresh cilantro

salt and freshly ground pepper to taste

3 cloves garlic, chopped

2 tablespoons Bragg Liquid Aminos

Method

1. Cook the barley according to package directions.

2. Mix the dressing ingredients and set aside.

3. Peel and dice 3 of the avocados.

4. In a large bowl, mix together the barley, diced avocados, kale, tomatoes, and two-thirds of the seeds. Add the dressing and combine well. Let the dressed salad sit for 30 minutes or more before serving, allowing flavors to combine.

5. Just before serving, peel and slice the remaining 2 avocados. Toss the salad, top it with the sliced avocados, and sprinkle with the remaining sunflower or sesame seeds.

Kale Dressed in Avocado

If you are someone who likes to play with your food, wash your hands and get busy. Massaging the kale actually tenderizes it, so don't skip this step.

Serves 6

Ingredients

2 avocados, mashed

juice of 1 large or 2 small lemons

2 cloves garlic, minced

2 tablespoons olive oil

2 bunches of kale, ribs removed, leaves finely shredded

1 small red onion, diced

2 fresh tomatoes, diced

salt and freshly ground pepper

Method

1. In the bottom of a large salad bowl, mix together the avocado, lemon juice, garlic, and oil.

2. Add the shredded kale and massage everything together with your fingers until the kale feels tender and the avocado evenly coats the leaves.

3. Add the onion, tomatoes, and salt and pepper to taste.

4. Toss well.

Avocado and Daikon with Lemon-Miso Dressing

This fresh and easy salad can be assembled in advance and tossed right before serving. Just remember to add the avocados at the last minute so they don't brown.

Serves 6 to 8

For the salad

½ pound arugula, stems trimmed

½ daikon radish, peeled and cut into matchstick strips

3 carrots, peeled and cut into matchstick strips

½ cup pumpkin seeds, toasted

2 avocados, peeled and cubed

1 bell pepper, orange or red, membrane and seeds removed, flesh cut into matchstick strips

For the dressing

3 tablespoons fresh lemon juice

1 tablespoon miso of your choice

1 tablespoon stone-ground mustard

3 tablespoons chopped parsley

2 tablespoons chopped cilantro

¼ cup olive oil

1½ tablespoons honey

3 tablespoons rice wine vinegar

salt and freshly ground pepper

Method

1. Mix the ingredients for the dressing in a small bowl.

2. Combine the salad ingredients in a large bowl.

3. Just before serving, dress and toss the salad.

Strawberry Fields Spinach Salad

There's a brief moment in late spring and early summer when spinach and strawberries are in season at the same time in the garden. Seize that opportunity to make this heavenly salad — an unusual and delicious combination of flavors and textures.

Serves 4

For the salad

½ cup pecans or sliced almonds

1 bunch spinach, tough stems trimmed

1 pint fresh strawberries, stems removed, berry hulled, and then sliced

For the dressing

2 tablespoons sesame seeds

1½ tablespoons maple syrup

1 tablespoon poppy seeds

¼ cup cider vinegar

½ cup grapeseed oil

1 tablespoon minced red onion

¼ teaspoon paprika

salt and freshly ground pepper to taste

2 tablespoons fresh lemon juice

Method

1. In a small pan over medium heat, toast the sesame seeds, stirring often.

2. Mix the dressing ingredients in a small bowl.

3. Toast the nuts in a pan, stirring often.

4. Combine the spinach, strawberries, and warm nuts. Add dressing to taste and toss lightly.

Potato and Pasta Medley

You might not think to pair pasta and potatoes until you've tried this recipe. Then just try to stop wanting more.

Serves 6

Ingredients

5 ounces pasta (we use a short ridged pasta)

6 medium-size red skin potatoes

salt

½ cup apple cider vinegar

¼ cup sugar

3 tablespoons grapeseed oil

½ teaspoon celery salt

¼ teaspoon freshly ground pepper

2 cups frozen peas, defrosted

1 medium red onion, finely chopped

1 orange bell pepper, chopped

¼ cup loosely packed fresh dill

¼ cup chopped flat-leaf parsley

4 stalks celery, chopped

½ cup cashews, toasted and chopped

½ cup Just Mayo

½ cup vegan sour cream

1 tablespoon Dijon mustard

Method

1. Bring a pot of salted water to a boil and cook the pasta according to the package directions while you prepare the other ingredients. When done, drain and set aside.

2. Place the potatoes in a pot and cover with cold water. Bring the water to a boil and cook over high heat. Season with salt, reduce the heat to medium, and cook until the potatoes are fork tender, 8 to 9 minutes. When done, remove from the heat, drain in a colander, and set aside to cool slightly.

3. While the pasta and potatoes cook, pour apple cider vinegar into a saucepan and bring to a boil. Add sugar and stir to dissolve. Turn off the heat.

4. While the potatoes are still slightly warm, cut them into ¾-inch cubes, leaving their skins on, and transfer to a large bowl. Pour the apple cider vinegar mixture over the warm potatoes. Drizzle in the grapeseed oil and stir in the celery salt and pepper.

5. Add the peas and pasta to the potatoes and toss. Add the onion, bell pepper, dill, parsley, celery, and cashews and stir everything together.

6. In another small bowl, mix the Just Mayo, sour cream, and Dijon mustard. Stir into the potato and macaroni mixture.

Serve at room temperature or chilled.

...ner Sweet Potato Salad

...at a sweet potato, do you think Thanksgiving? Think again. Low in calories and full ...e sweet potato offers an enticing alternative to conventional potato salad. Patty has been known to grab a few spoonfuls as a snack.

Serves 12

Ingredients

8 large sweet potatoes, peeled and cut into small chunks

2 tablespoons grapeseed oil

salt and freshly ground pepper to taste

1 teaspoon celery salt

2 tablespoons coarsely chopped fresh dill, plus more as needed

1 tablespoon Bragg Liquid Aminos

1 cup chopped scallions, white and green parts

½ cup Just Mayo

¼ cup vegan sour cream

Method

1. Preheat the oven to 375 degrees.

2. In a bowl, sprinkle the sweet potatoes with the grapeseed oil and season with salt and pepper, celery salt, dill, and Bragg. Toss to coat.

3. Spread the potatoes out on a parchment paper-lined baking sheet and bake until fork-tender.

4. Remove from the oven and let cool.

5. In a large bowl, stir together the scallions, Just Mayo, and sour cream.

6. Fold the potatoes into the dressing and toss to coat. Taste and add more dill, salt, and pepper, if desired.

Note
• Can refrigerate for up to 2 days.

Simply Dressed Beets

You can dress up your beets all kind of ways. (Just look at the Beet "Tartare" on page 35.) But there's also something to be said for simplicity, and a minimalist approach to a vegetable that is already so exceptional on its own, especially when it makes such a beautiful platter.

Serves 4 to 6

Ingredients

1½ bunches medium-size beets

½ medium red onion, thinly sliced

1 to 2 tablespoons olive oil

splash of Bragg Liquid Aminos

fresh dill, for garnish

Method

1. Preheat the oven to 350 to 375 degrees.

2. Wrap the beets in foil and roast on a baking sheet until tender, 45 minutes to 1 hour. Let cool, then peel and slice the beets.

3. In a bowl, combine the beets and the onion slices. Toss with the olive oil and Bragg, and sprinkle with fresh dill.

Note
• To save time, you can boil the beets for 30 to 45 minutes, but they won't be as sweet as roasted ones.

Grilled Romaine with Caesar Dressing

Legend has it that Caesar salad dates back to the early 1920s and an Italian chef who faced holiday shortages at a restaurant in Mexico. He made do with the ingredients he had, tossing the salad table side to add some panache. Those of us on a plant-based diet long ago figured out how to "veganize" the Caesar salad, but Diane often grills her romaine to add a smoky twist to this classic.

Serves 4

Prepare in advance

Nutty Parm, page 241

For the romaine

2 hearts of romaine

olive oil, for drizzling

salt and freshly ground pepper

2 cloves garlic, finely chopped

Nutty Parm, for sprinkling

croutons

For the dressing

Makes ¾ cup

5 tablespoons slivered almonds, toasted

2 tablespoons Dijon mustard

2½ tablespoons shoyu soy sauce or tamari

6 to 7 cloves garlic, roasted

3 tablespoons tahini

5 tablespoons fresh lemon juice

¼ cup extra-virgin olive oil

¼ cup water, or more if needed

1 tablespoon Worcestershire sauce

1 tablespoon nutritional yeast

2 tablespoons Nutty Parm

Method

1. To make the dressing, combine the almonds, mustard, shoyu, garlic, tahini, and lemon juice in a food processor or blender. Pulse until smooth.

2. While the blender is running, slowly add the oil, then the water and the Worcestershire, nutritional yeast, and Nutty Parm.

3. Cut each romaine heart in half lengthwise. Do not remove the cores. Season lightly with olive oil, garlic, salt, and pepper.

4. Cook the romaine on a hot grill or grill pan until just wilted and charred, being careful to avoid burning it.

5. Transfer the grilled romaine to a platter. Drizzle with Caesar dressing, sprinkle with Nutty Parm, and top with croutons.

Serve with extra dressing on the side.

Brussels Sprouts and Hijiki

Sea vegetables, common in Asian cuisines but barely used in this country, are one of the most nutritious foods you can eat, so we are always looking for new ways to bring them into our diet. Here hijiki is combined with shredded Brussels sprouts, sliced apples, and a dressing that is a perfect balance of salty, sour, and fruity. Once Diane made this, we all wanted it again and again. If you are looking for something light, healthy, and deliciously different, try this recipe.

Serves 6

For the salad

1 cup water

½ cup hijiki

1 teaspoon toasted sesame oil

5 scallions, 1 chopped, 4 sliced

1½ pounds brussel sprouts, trimmed

4 stalks celery, thinly sliced

1 green apple, skin on, thinly sliced

2 tablespoons chopped fresh mint

For the dressing

2 tablespoons shoyu soy sauce or tamari

2 tablespoons grapeseed oil

1 tablespoon umeboshi plum vinegar

juice of 1 lemon

juice of 1 orange

1 teaspoon Sriracha-style hot sauce

½ cup chopped flat-leaf parsley

¼ cup chopped cilantro

Method

1. Whisk together all the dressing ingredients.

2. In a small pot, bring 1 cup of water to a boil. Add the hijiki, sesame oil, and the chopped scallion. Cook on low heat approximately 10 minutes, until the hijiki is plump. Then drain.

3. Using a food processor with the thin slicing blade, slice the Brussels sprouts.

4. Transfer the shredded Brussels sprouts to a large bowl and add the sliced scallions, celery, hijiki, and apples.

5. Add the dressing to the salad and toss well to combine. Allow to marinate for 30 minutes before serving.

Note
• Umeboshi vinegar is quite salty, so no additional salt is needed for the dressing.
• Most sea vegetables are sold in dried form and need to be reconstituted, as in step 2.

Asian Slaw

Inspired by Deborah Madison's Asian Cobb Salad, Chef Diane turned the ingredients into a spicy, crunchy slaw. It's a place where East and West come together in a dish that transcends borders.

Serves 4 to 6

For the salad

2 cups thinly sliced spinach or Swiss chard leaves

2 cups thinly sliced Napa cabbage

2 cups thinly sliced red cabbage

1 large cucumber, peeled, seeded, and diced

4 scallions, white and green parts, thinly sliced on a diagonal

1 small black radish or turnip, cut into matchsticks

1 tablespoon black and/or white sesame seeds, toasted

For the dressing

2 cloves finely chopped garlic

4 tablespoons grapeseed oil

3 tablespoons rice wine vinegar

1½ tablespoons mirin

1 tablespoon hot sesame oil

1 tablespoon shoyu soy sauce or tamari

½ jalapeño pepper, seeded and minced finely

1 tablespoon tahini

6 fresh mint leaves, finely chopped

2 tablespoons chopped fresh cilantro

1 tablespoon chopped Thai or cinnamon basil

Method

1. Put the dressing ingredients in a blender or food processor and blend well.

2. Put the salad ingredients in a large bowl.

3. Toss salad with dressing. Allow to marinate at least 30 minutes before serving.

Note
• Can refrigerate dressing for several days.
• Dressing also freezes well.

Red Cabbage Salad
with Maple-Glazed Walnuts

If you can take some time in advance to glaze the walnuts and prepare the Artisanal Feta Cheese, the salad itself comes together quickly and impressively. Plus you'll have leftover cheese to add to other dishes or to freeze, and maybe a few extra maple walnuts for snacking.

Serves 6 to 8

Prepare in advance

Maple-Glazed Walnuts, page 241

Artisanal Feta Cheese, page 18

For the salad

8 cups thinly sliced red cabbage

5 scallions, white and green parts, thinly sliced

1 cup Maple-Glazed Walnuts

⅓ cup crumbled Artisanal Feta Cheese

For the vinaigrette

⅓ cup extra-virgin olive oil

3 tablespoons red wine vinegar

2 cloves garlic, chopped

2 tablespoons Dijon mustard

2 tablespoons fresh dill

¼ teaspoon salt

¼ teaspoon freshly ground pepper

Method

1. Whisk together all the vinaigrette ingredients and set aside.

2. In a large bowl, combine the cabbage and scallions.

3. Toss the salad with the vinaigrette. Add half the walnuts and half the feta and toss again.

4. Top the salad with the remaining walnuts and feta and serve.

Quinoa Tabbouleh

For a high-protein, gluten-free version of this classic Middle Eastern salad, we use quinoa instead of cracked wheat. Tabbouleh lends itself to many variations in seasonings and presentations; improvise depending on what you have on hand, but do include some umeboshi plum vinegar for its unique salty-sweet-fruity-sour flavor. Serve mounded in a serving bowl or stuffed in tomatoes.

Serves 6

Prepare in advance

Artisanal Feta Cheese, page 18 (optional)

Ingredients

1 cup quinoa, rinsed several times

2 medium tomatoes, diced

½ cup finely sliced celery

1 green bell pepper, finely chopped

1 cucumber, peeled, seeded, and finely chopped

¼ to ½ cup finely chopped scallions

salt and freshly ground pepper to taste

½ cup fresh-squeezed lemon juice

4 cloves garlic, finely chopped

¼ cup chopped fresh mint

¼ cup olive oil

1 cup chopped flat-leaf parsley

1 tablespoon Bragg Liquid Aminos

¼ cup chopped fresh cilantro

2 tablespoons rice wine vinegar

1 tablespoon umeboshi plum vinegar

Artisanal Feta Cheese (optional garnish)

Method

1. Cook the quinoa according to package directions.

2. Meanwhile, combine the other ingredients in a large bowl.

3. When the quinoa is cooked, drain any remaining water. Add the quinoa to the bowl with the other ingredients and mix thoroughly but gently.

4. Refrigerate for several hours before serving. Sprinkle with Artisanal Feta cheese, if desired.

Note
• It's fine to use leftover quinoa to make tabbouleh.

Cucumbers & Watermelon

Serves 4

Savory Watermelon Olive Salad

Serves 4 to 6

Here are two very different salads, both featuring watermelon. One is savory, the other a little sweeter, but both are quick as can be and are prepared by just tossing the ingredients together.

Prepare in advance

Artisanal Feta Cheese, page 18

Ingredients

1 small red onion, thinly sliced, soaked in ice water with 1 teaspoon sugar for 30 minutes

3 cups chopped spicy greens (mustard, arugula, etc.)

1 cup finely chopped flat-leaf parsley

1 cup finely chopped fresh mint leaves

¼ cup finely chopped fresh cilantro

2 pounds seedless watermelon, cut into small chunks

6 plum tomatoes, cubed

20 pitted olives (Kalamata or oil-cured), halved

¼ cup Artisanal Feta Cheese

¼ cup olive oil

juice of 2 limes

salt and freshly ground pepper to taste

Ingredients

½ cup chopped fresh mint leaves

¼ cup chopped fresh Thai basil

2 pounds seedless watermelon, cut into small chunks

1 cup fresh cherries, pitted and halved, or dried cherries, halved

juice of 2 limes

1 cucumber, peeled, seeded, and cut into small chunks

2 tablespoons fresh chopped tarragon

¼ cup rice wine vinegar

salt and freshly ground pepper to taste

Spiced Cauliflower with Lentils and Dates

An unusual fusion of ingredients, this salad has a unique taste and substantial presence. It's nutritious, comforting, and satisfying enough to be a meal on its own.

Serves 6

Ingredients

1 cup French lentils, rinsed

¼ cup plus 3 tablespoons olive oil

½ small red onion, sliced

3 cloves garlic, chopped

4 cups chopped Swiss chard or greens of your choice

1 head cauliflower, cut into florets

¼ teaspoon ground cumin

¼ teaspoon ground cinnamon

¼ teaspoon ground ginger

pinch of cayenne pepper

1 bunch scallions, chopped

salt and freshly ground pepper to taste

2 tablespoons tahini

3 tablespoons fresh-squeezed lemon juice

1 teaspoon honey

2 tablespoons water

½ cup raw almonds, toasted

10 dates, pitted and chopped

Method

1. Cook the lentils according to package directions. Let cool.

2. Heat 1 tablespoon of the olive oil in a large pan and sauté the onion and garlic until soft. Stir in the Swiss chard and cook until wilted. Set aside and let cool.

3. On a baking sheet, toss the cauliflower florets with ¼ cup of the olive oil, the cumin, cinnamon, ginger, cayenne, scallions, and salt and pepper to taste. Roast for 20 minutes in a 425-degree oven until the cauliflower is tender and golden brown. Take care not to overcook the cauliflower.

4. In a large bowl, whisk the tahini, lemon juice, honey, remaining 2 tablespoons olive oil, and the water until smooth. Add the lentils, season with salt and pepper, and toss to coat.

5. Add the Swiss chard mixture, cauliflower, almonds, and dates to the bowl. Toss everything together so the ingredients are evenly distributed and serve.

Walnut Cranberry Salad

We love this salad as part of a cold weather holiday feast, or as a way to add something dazzling and colorful to a simpler meal. You can substitute oven-roasted grapes for the cranberries; use the same procedure for the grapes that is used for our Oven-Dried Tomatoes (page 243).

Serves 6

Ingredients

¾ cup apple cider

¼ cup apple cider vinegar

1 shallot, thinly sliced

½ cup grapeseed oil

¼ cup chopped flat-leaf parsley

2 tablespoons chopped fresh dill

1 cup walnuts, toasted

1 cup dried cranberries

1 small red onion, sliced

3 carrots, sliced or diced

3 heads romaine, shredded, or
8 to 10 cups of another lettuce

Method

1. To make the dressing, heat the apple cider in a saucepan until it reduces by half.

2. Add the cider vinegar, the shallot, grapeseed oil, parsley, and dill, and whisk to combine. Remove from the heat and let cool.

3. In a large bowl, mix together the walnuts, cranberries, red onion, carrots, and lettuce. Toss with the dressing.

Lunch

Rainbow Shoots seen from the upper terrace.
Sculpture by Tom Gottsleben,
crystal glass, stainless steel, and glass aggregate

Can't Be Beet Sliders with Pickled Onions

Who doesn't love a juicy slider served on a bun — or as we sometimes like to do — on a grilled portobello. Here, grilled beets take center stage. We like our sliders slathered with spicy horseradish mustard and dripping with pickled onions (our homemade version is on page 244).

Serves 6

Prepare in advance

Pickled Onions, page 244

For the sandwich

4 medium-size beets

4 toasted rolls or 4 grilled portobello mushrooms

lettuce leaves

pickled onions

spicy horseradish mustard

For the marinade

10 peppercorns

1 teaspoon chopped fresh rosemary

1 teaspoon whole fennel seed

2 bay leaves

4 cloves garlic, peeled

1 teaspoon smoked paprika

1 teaspoon chopped fresh thyme

1 heaping tablespoon granulated garlic

¼ cup Worcestershire sauce

⅓ cup ketchup

¼ cup beet cooking water

2 tablespoons maple syrup

Method

1. Boil the whole beets in water until tender, up to 60 minutes, then drain, reserving ¼ cup of the cooking water for the marinade.

2. Run the cooked beets under cold water and the skin will peel right off.

3. Slice the peeled beets thickly and put them in a large bowl.

4. In a small bowl, stir together the ingredients for the marinade, then add to the beets. Let the beets marinate for 30 minutes or longer.

5. Preheat a grill to medium-high heat. Grill the beet slices and portobello mushrooms, if using, turning once.

6. Serve beets on a toasted roll or grilled portobello, layering the beets with a lettuce leaf, some pickled onions, and spicy horseradish mustard.

Black Bean and Corn Burger

If you find a better bean burger than this one, you let us know. We mean it! On top of a portobello mushroom cap or inside a bun, this version has a substantial texture and depth of flavor that is everything we think one could want in a burger. Our recipe is enough to feed a crowd; you can easily cut it in half, or freeze the extras for future use.

Makes 18 burgers

For the burgers

2 (15-ounce) cans black beans, drained and rinsed

1 cup cashews, toasted

4 cloves garlic, minced

3 large ears grilled corn, kernels removed; *or* 2 cups frozen corn kernels, defrosted

1 large red bell pepper, diced

1 teaspoon ground cumin

2 tablespoons chopped fresh cilantro

½ cup chopped flat-leaf parsley

2 teaspoons Bragg Liquid Aminos

2 teaspoons Pickapeppa Sauce

1 medium red onion, minced

¼ teaspoon salt, or to taste

¼ teaspoon freshly ground pepper

3 tablespoons ketchup

1 cup bread crumbs *or* 1 cup rolled oats, pulsed to bread crumb consistency

1 teaspoon Worcestershire sauce

For the portobellos

portobello mushrooms or buns

grapeseed oil, for brushing mushrooms

salt, pepper, and granulated garlic, for seasoning

Method

1. Preheat the oven to 350 degrees.

2. In food processor, pulse the beans and cashews.

3. In a large bowl, combine the bean mixture with the remaining burger ingredients. Mix well.

4. Using a spoon or ice cream scooper, scoop the bean mixture onto a parchment-lined baking sheet, flattening slightly to form each scoop into a nice burger shape. The burgers tend to spread when they cook, so don't make them too big. Bake for 20 to 25 minutes, turning halfway through.

5. While the burgers bake, remove the stems from the mushrooms, if using, and clean the caps with a slightly dampened cloth.

6. Brush the mushrooms with grapeseed oil and sprinkle with salt, pepper, and granulated garlic.

7. On a stovetop grill pan over medium heat, grill the mushrooms, cap side down, approximately 10 minutes.

8. When the mushrooms are softened and juicy, turn and grill them a little while longer. Serve each burger on top of a mushroom cap.

Note
• Why not make a platter with some burgers on buns and some on portobellos? This gives gluten-free folks a delicious option without your having to seek out gluten-free rolls.
• Unbaked burgers freeze well.

able Muffaletta

...eans sandwich works equally well at home for lunch, on-the-go for a picnic, or at an event ... crowd. For one Spiral House party, Diane set a six-foot-long muffaletta, a variation on this re... pe, sliced into individual servings, along the middle of the table as the centerpiece. It was devoured in astonishingly quick order by vegans and meat-eaters alike. Our resident native New Orleanian, designer Ronnie Shushan, said of the sandwich: "I liked Diane's version even better than the one from Central Grocery on Decatur Street. Frankly, it surprised me; I'm not even a vegetarian. It reminded me of the power of fresh whole food over something processed — even in a muffaletta."

Serves 6; triple the recipe to fill a 6-foot loaf

Prepare in advance

Nutty Parm, page 241

Artisanal Feta Cheese, page 18 (optional)

Ingredients

¼ cup olive oil

1 large or 2 medium heads cauliflower, sliced top to bottom in thick slabs

2 red bell peppers, sliced

2½ cups sliced pitted olives (we mix ½ cup oil-cured, 1 cup Kalamata, and 1 cup green Sicilian)

¼ cup finely chopped garlic

1 (4-ounce) jar pimientos

6 tablespoons capers, drained

½ cup thinly sliced celery

¼ cup finely chopped scallion

¼ cup chopped fresh basil

¼ cup chopped parsley

½ teaspoon hot pepper flakes

2 cucumbers, peeled, thinly sliced

4 small tomatoes, thinly sliced

Nutty Parm

A crusty loaf of bread (ciabatta, peasant bread, French bread, etc.) with some of the middle hollowed out

Method

1. Drizzle oil on the cauliflower and peppers and grill or roast them.

2. Make the olive salad by combining the next 10 ingredients in a bowl.

3. Spread olive salad on both sides of the bread. Add layers of roasted vegetables, then slices of cucumber and tomato. Add our plant-based feta cheese, if using, on top, and sprinkle with Nutty Parm.

4. Close the sandwich and cover with parchment paper. Place a cutting board on top of the sandwich and put something heavy like a book or a brick on top for two hours. This resting stage is important to allow time for the bread to absorb the juices.

5. Wrap in deli paper if you like, and cut into pieces.

Reuben Sandwich with Russian Dressing

We make no apology for having two plant-based versions of this beloved sandwich, said to have originated at New York City's famed Reuben's Restaurant and Delicatessen. (Our Smoky Beet Reuben follows on the next page.) As if two weren't enough — it wasn't for us — check out the Filo Reuben appetizer on page 22.

Makes 6 sandwiches

Prepare in advance

Russian Dressing, page 227

Ingredients

Earth Balance Organic Whipped Buttery Spread

12 slices of rye bread or bread of your choice

1 (16-ounce) jar sauerkraut, drained, rinsed, and mixed with ½ cup Russian Dressing

6 dairy-free cheese slices

3 avocados, pitted and sliced

3 or 4 fresh sliced tomatoes

Method

1. Preheat a skillet over medium heat.

2. Spread Earth Balance on one side of bread and place it, buttery side down, on the skillet.

3. Layer some of the sauerkraut mixture, cheese, sliced avocado, and sliced tomato on the bread.

4. Top with another slice of bread and spread Earth Balance on the outside. Repeat for each sandwich.

5. Grill sandwiches about 8 minutes, then turn and grill 8 minutes more, or until cheese melts. Repeat.

Smoky Beet Reuben

New York City may have given birth to the Reuben sandwich, but Montreal and the West Coast were quick to tailor it to their tastes. So why not a Smoky Beet Reuben from Saugerties in upstate New York, home to the Spiral House, the 1994 Woodstock Festival, and also the childhood home of comedian Jimmy Fallon?

Makes 6 sandwiches

Prepare in advance

Russian Dressing, page 227

For the sandwich

3 or 4 large beets

salt and freshly ground pepper

12 slices of rye bread or bread of your choice

Earth Balance Organic Whipped Buttery Spread

1 cup non-dairy Russian Dressing

1½ cups sauerkraut, drained and rinsed

For the marinade

10 peppercorns

1 teaspoon chopped fresh rosemary

1 teaspoon whole fennel seed

2 bay leaves

4 cloves garlic, peeled

1 teaspoon smoked paprika

1 teaspoon chopped fresh thyme

1 heaping tablespoon granulated garlic

¼ cup Worcestershire sauce

⅓ cup ketchup

½ cup beet cooking water

2 tablespoons maple syrup

Method

1. Boil the whole beets in water until tender, then drain, reserving ½ cup cooking water.

2. Peel the beets, slice them 1 to 1½ inches thick, and put them in a large bowl.

3. In a small bowl, mix together the ingredients for the marinade, then add to the beets. Let beets marinate for 30 minutes or longer.

4. Grill or roast the beets, 5 minutes on each side.

5. Spread Earth Balance on one side of bread, then place on the grill, buttery side down. Layer some Russian dressing, beets, then sauerkraut, then more Russian dressing. Top with a second slice of bread.

6. Spread Earth Balance on the top piece of bread and grill the sandwich, turning to brown both sides. Repeat.

Open-Face Cauliflower Sandwich

You can't possibly imagine how good such a simple thing could be until you have eaten it. The seasoned cauliflower rub, aioli, and roasted red pepper combine to turn a familiar vegetable into the star of a favorite sandwich.

Serves 6

Prepare in advance

Roasted Red Peppers, page 242

Aioli, page 226; or Roasted Garlic, page 242

Nutty Parm (optional), page 241

For the rub

½ teaspoon dried oregano

½ teaspoon ground white pepper

½ teaspoon freshly ground pepper

¼ teaspoon dried thyme

½ teaspoon Italian seasoning

½ teaspoon celery salt

½ teaspoon ground turmeric

½ teaspoon smoked paprika

1 teaspoon granulated garlic

1 teaspoon onion powder

½ teaspoon salt

For the sandwich

2 small or 1 large head cauliflower, sliced from the top of the head through the stem, making one large slab for each sandwich

olive oil, to coat cauliflower

Aioli, or roasted garlic and Just Mayo

6 slices bread of your choice

3 tomatoes, sliced

2 roasted red bell peppers, sliced or 1½ cups if using jarred peppers

Nutty Parm (optional)

Method

1. Preheat the oven to 400 degrees.

2. Mix the rub ingredients together and set aside.

3. On an oiled baking sheet, place the cauliflower slices in a single layer.

4. Coat each slice first with the rub and then with the olive oil.

5. Roast for 25 to 30 minutes, turning cauliflower halfway through. Remove from oven when lightly browned.

6. To assemble sandwich, spread Aioli on each slice of bread, followed by a tomato slice, a slice of roasted cauliflower, then a few red pepper slices. Top with Nutty Parm, if desired.

~andwich
~obello, Lettuce, and Tomato)

Th~s ~ ~been veganized with such perfection you may find it difficult to remember what attraction the original ever held. Our version is both filling and faultless.

Serves 6

For the marinade

3 cloves garlic, minced

4 to 5 dashes of liquid smoke

½ cup grapeseed oil

freshly ground pepper and smoked salt, to taste

For the dressing

½ cup Just Mayo

3 to 4 fresh basil leaves, rolled and cut in thin strips

2 scallions, finely chopped

2 cloves garlic, finely chopped

freshly ground pepper, to taste

2 teaspoons Bragg Liquid Aminos

2 tablespoons fresh lemon juice

½ cup vegan sour cream

2 teaspoons Sriracha-style hot sauce

2 tablespoons finely chopped cilantro

For the sandwich

3 portobello mushrooms

12 slices bread of your choice

lettuce leaves

3 tomatoes, sliced

2 cucumbers, peeled and sliced (optional)

Method

1. Whisk together the marinade ingredients and set aside.

2. Whisk together the dressing ingredients, mixing well and seasoning to taste.

3. Clean the mushroom caps (discard stems or save for stock). Toss caps with marinade and let sit for at least 1 hour.

4. On an outdoor grill or stovetop grill pan, grill mushrooms until tender, 8 to 10 minutes.

5. Cut mushrooms into strips.

6. Toast bread.

7. Spread dressing on bread and layer lettuce, sliced tomato, and mushroom strips. For more crunch, add sliced cucumber.

Better-than-Chicken Salad

The key to this un-chicken salad is a product from Beyond Meat, a young company with high-profile investors; you'll find more about them on page 267. In this dish, we combine their grilled Beyond Chicken strips with toasted cashews and a Dijon-herb dressing for a quick salad that will satisfy on a sandwich or atop a bed of lettuce.

Serves 3 to 4

Ingredients

1 (9-ounce) package "Beyond Chicken" Grilled Strips; if frozen, defrost at room temperature for approximately 30 minutes

1 cup raw cashews

4 stalks celery, chopped

1 cup seedless grapes, sliced in half

1 tablespoon chopped flat-leaf parsley

½ tablespoon chopped fresh dill

½ tablespoon chopped fresh tarragon

¾ cup dried cranberries

¾ cup vegan sour cream

4 tablespoons Just Mayo

1 teaspoon Dijon mustard

½ teaspoon celery salt

lettuce, for serving

Note
• Do not actually cook the defrosted "chicken" strips; just warm them.
• To serve as a sandwich, chop the ingredients more finely.

Method

1. Steam the Beyond Chicken strips until just warm, then chop and put in a bowl.

2. Toast the cashews in a sauté pan and add them to the bowl.

3. Mix in the remaining ingredients and serve scoops of the salad on beds of lettuce

Bubbe's Potato Pancakes

No doubt your Jewish *bubbe* has cornered the market on potato *latkes*, but we are delighted to say we have a recipe that would still make her proud. This dish will elevate you to the ranks of a true *balabusta* (the Yiddish expression for good homemaker). It's as good as anything you will find along New York's Lower East Side and as authentic in taste as any *latke* served during the Hanukkah festival.

Serves 6

Ingredients

3 pounds russet potatoes

1 medium yellow onion, grated

1 tablespoon chopped fresh parsley

¼ cup all-purpose flour

½ teaspoon baking powder

1 teaspoon salt

¼ teaspoon freshly ground pepper

grapeseed oil, for frying

for garnish:

vegan sour cream

apple sauce

chopped scallions (optional)

2 flax eggs (1 flax egg = 1 tablespoon flaxseed soaked in 3 tablespoons warm water for 5 minutes)

Method

1. Peel and cut the potatoes in big pieces and put them in a bowl of cold water. When ready to grate, dry the potatoes with a dish towel to remove the excess liquid. Grate the potatoes by hand or in a food processor.

2. In a large bowl, mix together the potatoes, onion, parsley, flour, baking powder, salt, and pepper.

3. Preheat the oven to 275 degrees.

4. In a large skillet, heat about 3 tablespoons of oil on medium-high. Be mindful that it doesn't burn. Scoop up a large soup spoon of the potato mixture, drop it into the pan, and flatten slightly with a fork. Without crowding, quickly add additional pancakes to the skillet. Cook until golden brown, turning once, approximately 4 minutes on each side.

5. As the pancakes finish cooking, transfer them to a cooling rack on top of a baking sheet. Place in the oven to keep warm until all the pancakes have been cooked.

Note
• Don't skip drying water from the potatoes. It's the difference between crisp and soggy pancakes.
• Frying temperature is also critical. To test that the oil is hot enough to fry the pancakes, put the end of a wooden spoon into the oil, the oil should bubble around the spoon.

chy Lettuce Wraps

rtually fat-free fare, these colorful wraps are enormously satisfying. Their simplicity
c...   ding — It does take a bit of time to chop the ingredients and assemble each piece, so
plan ahead. Ur, for a more informal presentation, prepare the ingredients in advance and let your
guests or children wrap their own, with or without the leek ties. Serve with a hot or cold soup.

Serves 4 to 6

Prepare in advance

Ginger-Tamari Dipping Sauce, page 225

Ingredients

2 heads Bibb or buttercrunch lettuce,
large outer leaves only

1 bunch asparagus, trimmed and peeled

1 daikon radish or jicama, peeled

1 lemon to make lemon water

½ package rice noodles, cooked
according to package directions

1 bunch scallions, finely sliced

2 bell peppers, cut into matchsticks

½ pound snow peas, stem ends
removed, cut into matchsticks

1 tablespoon chopped fresh cilantro

hijiki seaweed, reconstituted (see
package directions)

2 leeks to tie up wraps (optional),
roots removed, cut in half lengthwise,
washed well, blanched, green parts
cut into ribbons (see photo top right;
extra ribbons allow for breakage)

Ginger-Tamari Dipping Sauce

Note
• You can cook the rice noodles in
advance. Spread them on a cookie
sheet in a thin layer.

Method

1. Carefully remove lettuce leaves, wash, and pat dry.

2. Blanch asparagus. Drain and set aside to cool.

3. Julienne the jicama, then immediately place in
   lemon water to cover, to prevent discoloration.

4. Spread out a lettuce leaf. Arrange ingredients
   along the center rib, starting with rice noodles.

5. Beginning with the edge closest to you, roll the
   lettuce and secure with a blanched leek.

6. Serve with Ginger-Tamari Dipping Sauce.

Peanut-Sesame Noodles

We think our version will beat the standard item at your favorite Chinese restaurant. We often serve them with Sautéed Greens with Herbs (page 172), a combination that divides us into two kinds of eaters — the ones who keep everything separate on their plates and the ones who like to mix it all together. Either way, the combination makes a satisfying meal that transcends culture and ethnicity.

Serves 6

Ingredients

1½ pounds noodles (see notes)

2 tablespoons coconut oil

2 tablespoons toasted sesame oil, plus more for tossing with noodles

1 tablespoon grated fresh ginger

3 cloves garlic, chopped

½ cup chopped scallions

¼ cup tahini

¾ cup peanut butter, chunky or creamy

3 tablespoons shoyu soy sauce or tamari, plus more for tossing with noodles

1 cup vegetable stock or cooking water from noodles

1 (13.5-ounce) can unsweetened coconut milk

2 tablespoons Siracha-style hot sauce, optional

3 tablespoons chopped fresh cilantro

toasted sesame seeds, snow peas, and/or chopped scallions, for garnish

Method

1. Cook the noodles according to package directions, reserving 1 cup water.

2. While the pasta cooks, heat the coconut and sesame oils in a sauté pan and sweat the ginger, garlic, and scallions.

3. Add the tahini, peanut butter, and tamari or shoyu.

4. Slowly pour in the vegetable stock or pasta water to the sauce, stirring to form a paste.

5. Add the coconut milk and hot sauce, if using. Stir to combine and remove from heat.

6. When the noodles are cooked to al dente, drain and spread them out on a baking sheet, toss with a little sesame oil to prevent them from sticking together, and drizzle a little soy sauce over the noodles. You can let the noodles sit while you prepare the rest of your meal, and then toss with the sauce just before serving.

7. Toss the noodles with peanut sauce and cilantro.

8. Garnish with toasted sesame seeds, snow peas, and/or scallions.

Note
• We generally use quinoa spaghetti for our peanut noodles. Pure buckwheat soba would be another gluten-free option, or soba noodles (not gluten-free).
• The treatment of the noodles in step 6 is the key to having noodles that don't get gummy.
• Finished dish refrigerates well.
• **Sauce freezes** well.
• Can be served hot or at room temperature.

Tomato Pie

These tasty little tomato pies are guaranteed to delight. The fresh garden tomatoes are enhanced with two veganized ingredients that you see often in our recipes — our ricotta cheese and our plant-based Parmesan. This is a good one for finicky eaters. And everyone else, too.

Makes 6 mini pies or one 9-inch pie

Prepare in advance

Nutty Parm, page 241

Artisanal Ricotta Cheese, page 18

Ingredients

4 slices hearty bread, lightly toasted

⅓ cup Nutty Parm, plus more for topping

¼ cup chopped fresh basil

¼ cup chopped flat-leaf parsley

½ teaspoon chopped fresh thyme

salt and freshly ground pepper to taste

1 stick Earth Balance Vegan Buttery Stick

¼ cup Artisanal Ricotta Cheese

2 or 3 ripe, fresh tomatoes, sliced

Method

1. Preheat the oven to 375 degrees.

2. In a food processor, pulse the bread to make bread crumbs. Transfer to a large bowl and stir in the Nutty Parm and the herbs. Season with salt and pepper to taste.

3. Melt the Earth Balance and stir it into the bread crumb mixture.

4. Press the bread crumb mixture into the bottom and sides of 6 ramekins or a pie plate.

5. Bake for 8 minutes.

6. Remove from the oven and add a layer of ricotta cheese, followed by a layer of tomato slices.

7. Reduce the oven temperature to 325 degrees, and bake for 30 to 45 minutes, until the tomatoes are charred and the bread crumb crusts are golden brown. Check after 30 minutes.

8. Top with Nutty Parm and serve.

Note
• Use only fresh garden tomatoes for this recipe.

Zucchini Feta Pancakes

Our take on this Middle Eastern standard will be impossible to differentiate from the conventional version that is held together with eggs. Once again, "flax eggs" come to the rescue.

Makes 24 to 30 pancakes, 3-inches in diameter, which serves 8 for lunch

Prepare in advance

Basic Cashew Cream, page 220

Artisanal Feta Cheese, page 18

Ingredients

8 cups peeled and coarsely grated zucchini

2 medium-size russet potatoes, peeled and coarsely grated

3 flax eggs (1 flax egg = 1 tablespoon flaxseed soaked in 3 tablespoons warm water for 5 minutes)

2 tablespoons grapeseed oil for sautéing, plus 3 more for frying

1 tablespoon Earth Balance Vegan Buttery Stick

1 onion, diced

3 cloves garlic, chopped

1 cup Basic Cashew Cream

2 cups Artisanal Feta Cheese

salt and ground white pepper, to taste

2 tablespoons Bragg Liquid Aminos

1 tablespoon chopped fresh dill

¾ cup all-purpose flour

½ teaspoon ground turmeric

1 teaspoon ground cumin

preserves, sour cream, horseradish, and/or apple sauce (optional garnishes)

Method

1. Put the grated zucchini in a colander set over a bowl. Cover the zucchini with a clean kitchen towel and press canned beans or another weight on top to remove excess moisture.

2. In a large bowl, stir together the drained zucchini, potato, and flax eggs.

3. Heat 2 tablespoons grapeseed oil and 1 table-spoon Earth Balance, add onion and garlic, and sauté until soft. Add to the zucchini mixture.

4. Stir in the cashew cream and then add the crumbled feta, a sprinkle of white pepper, Bragg, dill, flour, turmeric, and cumin. Stir to combine.

5. In a cast-iron skillet, heat 3 tablespoons oil (more if needed). Scoop up a large soup spoon of mix, drop it into the pan, and flatten slightly with the back of a spoon or a spatula. Without crowding, quickly add additional pancakes to the pan. Cook until browned and crispy, turning once, approximately 4 minutes per side.

6. As the pancakes finish cooking, transfer to a cooling rack placed over a baking sheet to drain.

7. Blot gently with paper towel to remove excess oil.

Serve hot with preserves, sour cream, horseradish, or apple sauce — or all of the above.

Note
• We like to use tromboncino squash from our garden for these pancakes because of their low moisture content. If you're buying zucchini at the market, small ones have less moisture than large ones. If you have large ones, they'll do fine if you press out all the moisture as instructed in step 1.

The
Chef's
Birthday
Lunch

Birthdays are special events at the Spiral House. Everyone picks their favorite lunch in advance and Chef Diane whips it up. So what happens when it's Diane's birthday? She selects the menu and the kitchen/garden crew prepares it. For Diane, we even use a tablecloth with real flatware and dishes instead of the plant-based disposables that we use everyday. Diane generally chooses a variation of one of her recipes — as was the case with her enchilada-casserole birthday lunch pictured here. And since it's her birthday, she doesn't have to write down the recipe once the meal is over. She just gets to enjoy it — as do we all.

Entrées

Rainbow Patty
Sculpture by Tom Gottsleben,
crystal glass, bluestone,
and stainless steel

Savory Galette

Appealingly rustic in appearance, galettes make a stunning presentation. They work equally well for sweet and savory dishes, so once you've got the method in your repertoire, you can use them for whatever filling strikes your fancy. This is one of our favorites.

Serves 4 to 6

Prepare in advance

Artisanal Ricotta Cheese, page 18

Diane's Piecrust dough, sugar omitted, page 248

Nutty Parm, page 241

Oven-Dried Tomatoes, page 243

Ingredients

3 tablespoons grapeseed oil

2 large onions, sliced

2 bell peppers in assorted colors (red, yellow, or green), sliced

4 cloves garlic, chopped

1 teaspoon fresh oregano

1 teaspoon fresh thyme

salt and freshly ground pepper to taste

½ cup pine nuts, toasted

1 head radicchio, shredded

2 zucchini, sliced thin

½ pound mushrooms, trimmed and sliced

piecrust dough

½ cup chopped fresh basil

1 cup Artisanal Ricotta Cheese

½ cup Nutty Parm

1 cup oven-dried tomatoes

tomatoes, sliced, for garnish

4 tablespoons Earth Balance Vegan Buttery Stick, melted, or olive oil, for brushing

Method

1. In a large sauté pan, heat the grapeseed oil and sauté the onions until softened.

2. Add the bell peppers, garlic, oregano, and thyme, and season with salt and pepper. Sauté until soft, stirring occasionally.

3. Add the toasted pine nuts, radicchio, zucchini, and mushrooms and continue to sauté. When softened, remove from heat and let cool a bit.

4. Preheat the oven to 375 degrees.

5. Roll out the dough between two pieces of parchment paper into a 9-inch round. Transfer the dough to a baking sheet or a pizza pan.

6. Spread the sautéed vegetables in the center of the dough, leaving a border of exposed crust all the way around, about 1½-inches wide. Top the vegetables with chopped basil and ricotta, sprinkle Nutty Parm over that, and add the oven-dried tomatoes as the top layer.

7. Gently fold the outer border of crust over the outer edge of the filling, leaving the center of the filling exposed, as shown in the photo. Garnish with sliced fresh tomatoes.

8. Brush the crust with melted Earth Balance, and bake the galette for 30 to 40 minutes until crust is golden brown.

9. Carefully transfer the baked galette to a serving platter.

Eggplant Rollatini

This dish will wow family or guests with both its appearance and flavor, yet it's relatively easy to make, and will last for up to two days. Even people who aren't keen on eggplant seem to like it.

Serves 4

Prepare in advance

Nutty Parm, page 241

Roasted Garden Marinara Sauce, page 230

Ingredients

1 cup Nutty Parm, plus more for topping

½ cup roughly chopped flat-leaf parsley

½ cup roughly chopped fresh basil

½ cup water

¼ cup finely chopped pitted Kalamata olives

salt and freshly ground pepper to taste

2 eggplants, 1 pound each, peeled, sliced lengthwise ¼- to ½-inch thick (making about 10 slices total)

olive oil, for brushing

3 to 4 cups Roasted Garden Marinara Sauce

Method

1. Preheat the oven to 350 degrees.

2. In a food processor, combine Nutty Parm, parsley, and basil with the water. Process to a thin paste.

3. Transfer the paste to a bowl and stir in the olives. Season with salt and pepper to taste.

4. Heat the grill to medium-high. Brush the eggplant slices with olive oil and grill, turning once, until tender and lightly charred, 2 to 3 minutes. Alternatively, use a stovetop grill pan.

5. Arrange the grilled eggplant slices on a work surface and season with salt and pepper.

6. Spoon 1 tablespoon or more of the Nutty Parm herb filling onto one end of each eggplant slice and roll tightly so the filling is evenly distributed.

7. Place the eggplant rolls on an oiled baking pan, seam side down. Bake for 15 to 20 minutes.

8. Heat the marinara sauce. Spoon a layer of sauce on the bottom of each plate and arrange the eggplant rolls on top of the sauce.

9. Sprinkle with Nutty Parm and serve.

Note
• If making in advance, you can complete the recipe through step 5 and refrigerate. Wait to add the filling until you are ready to bake the dish.

Mushroom-Quinoa Risotto Cakes

The rich, buttery flavor of shiitake mushrooms and nutritional power of the quinoa make this entrée as substantial as it is elegant. Even though these cakes will disappear faster than the amount of time it took them to arrive on the table, they are well worth the effort. We serve them as an entrée, but a single cake makes a beautiful appetizer as well.

Makes 16 cakes, serving 8 as an entrée

Prepare in advance

Nutty Parm, page 241

Roasted Pepper and Tomato Confit, page 226

1 small butternut squash, cooked and puréed

Roasted Vegetable Stock, page 246 (if using homemade, or see notes)

Ingredients

¼ cup dried porcini mushrooms

2 large shallots, chopped

1½ cups chopped fresh shiitake mushroom caps, stems removed and added to vegetable stock to simmer

2 tablespoons Earth Balance Vegan Buttery Stick

1 cup quinoa, rinsed well three times

1 cup puréed butternut squash

½ cup dry white wine or water

2 cups mushroom water combined with vegetable stock

½ cup Nutty Parm

½ cup chopped flat-leaf parsley

salt and freshly ground pepper to taste

Method

1. Cover the dried porcini mushrooms with hot water. Let soften, 5 to 10 minutes, then drain, reserving the soaking liquid. Remove the stems and chop the mushrooms.

2. In a large pot, sauté the shallots, porcini, and shiitakes in Earth Balance until the mushrooms begin to brown, approximately 5 minutes.

3. Add the quinoa and cook until glossy and coated with the Earth Balance.

4. Add the wine and bring to a simmer, stirring occasionally until the liquid evaporates.

5. Combine all the reserved mushroom water with enough vegetable stock to equal 2 cups of liquid.

6. Continue cooking until the liquid is absorbed, 20 to 30 minutes. The quinoa should be creamy and starchy, which helps the cakes hold together. Turn off the heat.

7. Fold the squash into the quinoa. Add the Nutty Parm and parsley and stir to combine. Season with salt and pepper. Remove pot from heat.

8. Lightly oil a griddle and preheat it to medium-high. Using an ice cream scoop, spoon about ¼ cup of the quinoa mixture onto the pan, and flatten to make a patty about 1-inch thick. Without crowding, repeat with the additional quinoa patties. Cook until lightly brown and crispy, turning once, about 8 minutes per side.

9. Serve the quinoa cakes with Roasted Pepper and Tomato Confit.

Note
• If you don't have any homemade vegetable stock, add the mushroom stems to a cup or 2 of store-bought stock and simmer while you prepare the quinoa. In step 5, you can add this stock to your mushroom soaking water to make a total of 2 cups liquid.
• Freezes well, cooked or uncooked.

Puréed Cauliflower with Swiss Chard and Tempeh

A fermented soy product, tempeh is a versatile plant protein that is less processed than tofu. Boiling the tempeh removes a slight bitterness that many people find distasteful, and also softens it so it will absorb the flavors of the marinade or seasonings. We encourage you to try both of our tempeh entrées — the quickly prepared one here, perfect for a weeknight supper, and the somewhat fancier offering on the following pages.

Serves 6

Ingredients

2 medium-large heads cauliflower, cut into chunks

9 cloves garlic, 3 whole, 6 chopped

fresh parsley, ½ cup whole leaves, ¼ cup chopped

3 tablespoons cashew milk, or any unflavored non-dairy milk

1 tablespoon Earth Balance Buttery Stick

salt and freshly ground pepper to taste

3 bunches Swiss chard, stems removed and reserved, leaves rolled and shredded

4 to 5 tablespoons grapeseed oil, half for sautéing the cauliflower, half for the tempeh

1 large onion, chopped

2 (8-ounce) packages tempeh, cut into small cubes

1½ tablespoons fresh thyme *or* ½ teaspoon dried thyme

2 teaspoons dried oregano

Method for the cauliflower

1. In a large pot of boiling salted water, add the cauliflower and cook until tender. Drain.

2. Place cauliflower in a food processor. Pulse a few times, then add the 3 whole garlic cloves, the parsley leaves, cashew milk, and Earth Balance. Process until very smooth. Season with salt and pepper.

For the Swiss chard

1. Finely chop the chard stems.

2. In a large sauté pan, heat half the oil and sauté the onion, half the chopped garlic, and the chard stems until soft. Add the chard leaves and cook until wilted. Season with salt and pepper.

For the tempeh

1. In a medium-size sauté pan, bring enough water to cover the tempeh cubes to a boil. Add the tempeh, turn down the heat, and cook uncovered for 15 minutes. Drain the tempeh.

2. In a bowl, mix the remaining chopped garlic, the ¼ cup chopped parsley, thyme, oregano, and salt and pepper to taste. Add the tempeh and toss.

3. In the same pan used to boil the tempeh, heat the remainder of the oil and sauté tempeh until brown on all sides, approximately 10 minutes.

4. On a plate, layer the puréed cauliflower and sautéed Swiss chard, and top with the tempeh.

Tempeh Madeira

Madeira is one of several wines that are fortified with brandy or pure alcohol during the fermentation process. Its complex flavor and intoxicating bouquet adds an elegant depth in cooking, and makes our Tempeh Madeira a good choice for a special meal.

Serves 6

Prepare in advance

Roasted Vegetable Stock (if using homemade), page 246

For the marinade

2 cloves garlic, minced

¼ cup shoyu soy sauce or tamari

2 bay leaves

For the tempeh

2½ cups water

2 (8-ounce) packages flax tempeh (or tempeh of your choice), cut into slabs

½ cup olive oil

2 cloves garlic, chopped

4 shallots, thinly sliced

½ pound wild mushrooms (an equal combination of shiitake and oyster mushrooms works well), stems discarded, caps thinly sliced

3 tablespoons all-purpose flour

1 tablespoon chopped flat-leaf parsley

1 tablespoon chopped fresh thyme

¼ cup white wine

¼ cup Madeira wine

2 cups vegetable stock

Method

1. In a medium-size bowl, stir together the marinade ingredients.

2. Bring the water to a boil in a small pot. Salt the water and return to a boil. Add the tempeh and simmer for 20 minutes on low heat.

3. Drain the tempeh and add to the marinade. Set aside for 30 minutes.

4. In a large sauté pan, heat the olive oil and add the garlic, shallots, and mushrooms. Cook over medium heat for approximately 5 minutes, or until the mushrooms brown.

5. Using a slotted spoon, add the tempeh to the pan, reserving the marinade, and sauté until lightly browned.

6. Add the flour, parsley, and thyme to the tempeh and gently stir to combine. Scrape up bits from the bottom of the pan.

7. Gradually add the white wine and Madeira, stirring to prevent the sauce from getting lumpy.

8. Stir in the vegetable stock and reserved marinade.

9. Reduce heat to low and let everything simmer together for 15 to 20 minutes, until consistency of sauce is like gravy, stirring every few minutes to prevent sticking.

Note
• You can make this dish with tofu, or with a combination of tofu and tempeh. To prepare the tofu, cut it into slabs, dust it with flour, and place on a parchment-lined baking sheet. Bake in a preheated 375-degree oven for 10 minutes. Turn over and bake for 10 minutes more. Set aside to cool, then marinate for 30 minutes. Press the marinade from tofu and continue with the recipe from step 5 onward.

Diane's Enchiladas

This oh, so Latin American dish has been tweaked to make it oh, so vegan. With all the goodness of beans, spinach, potatoes, and dairy-free cheddar wrapped up inside each corn tortilla, it's a hearty meal. It also freezes well, so we generally double the recipe. Enchilada happens to be the past participle of the Spanish verb *enchilar*, which literally means to season with chile pepper. Ours is relatively mild; feel free to turn up the heat in yours.

Serves 12

Prepare in advance

Enchilada Sauce, recipe on facing page

Ingredients

2 tablespoons olive oil, plus more for oiling the baking dish

2 large onions, chopped

6 cloves garlic, minced

2 cups sliced mushrooms

2 bell peppers, chopped

2 cups small-diced red skin potatoes

2 (15-ounce) cans pinto beans, drained

1 pound fresh spinach, chopped

2 tablespoons nutritional yeast

1 tablespoon ground cumin

2 to 4 tablespoons fresh lime juice

1 teaspoon kosher salt, or to taste

1 teaspoon granulated garlic

2 teaspoons chili powder, or to taste

2 smoked chipotle peppers in adobo sauce, chopped

12 tortillas

non-dairy cheddar cheese, shredded

non-dairy sour cream

chopped scallions and chopped cilantro, for garnish

Method

1. Preheat the oven to 350 degrees.

2. In a large skillet, heat oil over medium-low heat. Add the onions, garlic, and mushrooms and sauté for 5 to 6 minutes.

3. Add the bell peppers, potatoes, pinto beans, and spinach. Cook for 5 to 7 minutes, stirring occasionally.

4. Add the nutritional yeast, cumin, lime juice, salt, granulated garlic, chili powder, and chipotle peppers. Stir and adjust seasonings to taste.

5. Lightly toast the tortillas directly on the stovetop, or if using an electric stove, in a frying pan.

6. On a flat work surface, spoon the filling into the center of each tortilla and roll firmly.

7. Place tortillas seam side down in an oiled baking dish. Spoon the remaining enchilada filling over the tortillas. Spoon some Enchilada Sauce over that, and finally add a layer of shredded cheese.

8. Bake for 30 minutes.

9. Top each serving with more Enchilada Sauce, cheese, and/or sour cream. Garnish with chopped scallions and cilantro.

10. Serve extra Enchilada Sauce on the side.

Note
• Freezes well. Bake for 15 minutes and cool completely before freezing. To serve, defrost overnight in the refrigerator, bring to room temperature, and bake for 15 minutes or until heated through.

Enchilada Sauce

Makes 3 cups

Ingredients

2 cups tomatillos, husked

2 heads garlic, tops cut off

2 onions, quartered

olive oil

salt and pepper

8 ounces of canned green chiles

¼ cup chopped fresh cilantro

¼ cup chopped flat-leaf parsley

1 tablespoon smoked chipotle peppers

2 cups fresh spinach

2 cups soy creamer

Method

1. Place tomatillos, garlic, and onions on a parchment-lined baking sheet. Drizzle with oil and sprinkle with salt and pepper.

2. Roast for 30 minutes at 375 degrees. Remove from oven. Cool slightly; squeeze garlic cloves from their skins.

3. Transfer the roasted ingredients to a food processor; add the remaining ingredients, and blend until creamy.

Quintessential Mac and Cheese

Here you have everyone's favorite comfort food reinvented. Actually, Chef Diane reinvented it twice, once as the casserole shown here, and again as a bite-size appetizer described on page 24.

Serves 8 as an entrée, 12 as a side dish

Prepare in advance

Savory Cashew Cream Sauce, page 221

Nutty Parm, page 241 (optional)

Ingredients

1 pound quinoa shells or pasta of your choice

1 medium–large head cauliflower, cut into chunks

2 tablespoons Earth Balance Vegan Buttery Stick, plus 1 tablespoon more for greasing the casserole dish

1 medium-size onion, finely chopped

3 cloves garlic, finely chopped

2 cups Cashew Cream Sauce

7-ounces Jack-style non-dairy cheese, cubed

7-ounces Jalapeño Havarti or similar non-dairy cheese, cubed

1¼ to 2 cups soy creamer

2 tablespoons chopped flat-leaf parsley

2 tablespoons chopped fresh dill

2 pinches of ground nutmeg

salt and freshly ground pepper to taste

Nutty Parm or panko bread crumbs, for topping

Method

1. Cook the noodles in salted water until al dente and drain.

2. Meanwhile, blanch the cauliflower and drain.

3. Combine the noodles and cauliflower in a large bowl.

4. Preheat the oven to 350 degrees.

5. Melt 2 tablespoons of Earth Balance in a wide pan. Sauté the onions and garlic until soft. Add the cashew cream and cubed cheeses and stir. Continue cooking on low heat until everything is well combined.

6. Slowly add the soy creamer, stirring with a wooden spoon, until the cheese is melted and you have a creamy sauce. It should stick to the back of a wooden spoon, but not be so thick that you can't pour it. You might not need all the soy creamer to get this consistency.

7. Add the sauce, chopped parsley, dill, and nutmeg to the cauliflower-noodle mixture. Taste for salt and pepper. If the mixture seems too thick, add more soy creamer.

8. Grease the bottom of a casserole with Earth Balance. Spoon in the noodle mixture and top with Nutty Parm or panko bread crumbs.

9. Bake for 35 to 40 minutes. Let rest for 10 minutes before serving.

Note
• Can make ahead: Refrigerate unbaked casserole for 2 to 3 days.
• Freezes well.

Harvest-Time Delicata Squa

This dish will not only look beautiful on your holiday table, it can easily be mac
heated just before eating. For an entrée that's fairly easy to make, it will leave
It wouldn't hurt to have a few copies of the recipe on hand; be assured, people will as...

Serves 4 to 6

Ingredients

4 delicata squash, cut in half lengthwise, seeds left in until baked

salt and freshly ground pepper to taste

2 cups cooked wild rice from about ⅔ cup uncooked

2 tablespoons olive oil, plus more for greasing

2 medium onions, finely chopped

4 medium-size shallots, finely chopped

3 cloves garlic, chopped

5 stalks celery, chopped

1½ cups sliced shiitake mushroom caps

1½ cups sliced oyster mushroom caps (or other wild mushroom)

1 teaspoon dried thyme

¼ teaspoon dried sage (optional)

2 tablespoons maple syrup

½ cup raisins

1 cup dried cranberries

1 cup roughly chopped toasted pecans

Method

1. Preheat the oven to 350 degrees.

2. Line a baking sheet with parchment paper and grease the paper. Season the squash halves with salt and pepper. Bake, cut sides down, until soft, approximately 30 minutes.

3. Cook the wild rice according to the package directions.

4. Meanwhile, heat the olive oil in a large skillet. Add the onions, shallots, garlic, celery, and both types of mushrooms and sauté until the vegetables have softened and are slightly browned. You don't want them too dark because they will continue cooking in the oven.

5. Add the thyme, sage if using, wild rice, and maple syrup and stir until well combined. Season with salt and pepper to taste.

6. Stir in the raisins, cranberries, and toasted pecans; turn off the heat.

7. When the squash is done baking, scrape out the seeds and stringy fibers surrounding them. Fill each half with the rice mixture. Return to the oven to bake for another 20 minutes.

Note
• Baking with the seeds intact helps the squash hold its shape, resulting in a bigger, easier-to-fill cavity.

eitan Piccata

This elegant entrée was inspired by the Seitan Piccata at the famed Candle 79 in Manhattan, one of our all-time favorite vegan restaurants anywhere. Piccata translates to "piquant" and our zesty sauce definitely gets its kick from generous amounts of lemon juice and capers. This recipe also works well with portobello mushrooms or tofu (for a gluten-free dish) or Gardein Crispy Tenders (not gluten-free).

Serves 6

Ingredients

1 leek, roots and dark woody outer leaves discarded, whites and tender green part cut in half lengthwise

4 tablespoons olive oil, plus more to cook the seitan

4 tablespoons Earth Balance Vegan Buttery Stick, or more as needed

2 large shallots, thinly sliced

2 large cloves garlic, chopped

1½ pounds seitan cutlets

2 tablespoons all-purpose flour, plus more for dredging

2 tablespoons nutritional yeast

⅛ to ¼ cup capers

1 cup white wine

3 bunches spinach, washed and stemmed, large leaves cut in half

2 cups vegetable stock

1 bay leaf

½ cup chopped flat-leaf parsley, plus more for garnish

2 sprigs fresh thyme *or* ½ teaspoon dried

½ teaspoon ground turmeric

¾ cup fresh lemon juice (we like it lemony)

salt and freshly ground pepper to taste

1 lemon, thinly sliced, for garnish

Note
• Swiss chard can be substituted for spinach; cut leaves into quarters and sauté until just tender.

Method

1. Thinly slice the leek and swish slices around in a bowl of cold water, letting the dirt sink to the bottom. Remove leek pieces with a slotted spoon.

2. Heat 3 tablespoons of olive oil and the Earth Balance together in a wide heavy pan and sauté the leek, shallots, and garlic until tender and translucent, 6 to 7 minutes. Transfer to a bowl.

3. Cut the seitan cutlets into ½-inch-thick slices. Pat dry. Dredge the cutlets in flour, shaking off excess.

4. Add more olive oil and Earth Balance as needed to the sauté pan and heat over medium-high heat. Cook the cutlets in batches until crisp, a few minutes per side. Transfer the cutlets to a platter as you finish cooking.

5. Using the same pan, heat more olive oil and Earth Balance if needed. Return the shallots, leek, and garlic to the pan. Add the flour and nutritional yeast. Cook for 5 minutes, stirring to make a roux.

6. Add the capers and wine and cook, stirring, until the wine is reduced by about half.

7. While you are finishing the sauce, heat the remaining tablespoon of olive oil in another sauté pan and quickly wilt the spinach. Drain well on paper towels.

8. Add the stock, bay leaf, parsley, thyme, turmeric, and lemon juice to the sauce. Cook over low heat, stirring a bit until the sauce reduces and thickens.

9. Return the fried cutlets to the pan and cook over low heat for another 5 minutes to allow the cutlets to absorb the flavor of the sauce. Spoon the sauce over the cutlets as they cook.

10. Serve immediately with the sautéed spinach. Spoon some sauce from the pan on each plate and garnish with parsley and lemon slices.

Cauliflower, Red Lentil, and Rhubarb Dal

The unusual addition of rhubarb to a South Indian dal enhances the complex flavors and adds a pleasing tartness. The cauliflower makes it substantial enough to enjoy as an entrée. We are so fond of this unique twist that we freeze rhubarb stalks in the spring so we can enjoy this dish year-round.

Makes 4 to 6 servings

Prepare in advance

Roasted Vegetable Stock, page 246

Ingredients

1 small cauliflower head, separated into small florets

olive oil

1 tablespoon granulated garlic

1 teaspoon salt, plus more for roasting the cauliflower

½ teaspoon freshly ground pepper, plus more for roasting the cauliflower

3 tablespoons grapeseed oil

1 onion, chopped

1 tablespoon minced garlic

2 tablespoons minced fresh ginger

2 teaspoons whole cardamom seeds, toasted and ground (or ground cardamom)

1 tablespoon yellow or brown mustard seeds

2 whole cloves, toasted and ground

1 tablespoon ground turmeric

1 teaspoon ground cumin

3 or 4 rhubarb stalks (discard leaves, which are toxic), trimmed and outer stringy fiber removed, then thinly sliced (see notes)

1 cup dried red lentils, rinsed

1 quart vegetable stock

¼ cup chopped fresh cilantro, for garnish (optional)

Method

1. Preheat the oven to 375 degrees.

2. Toss the cauliflower with olive oil, the granulated garlic, and season with salt and pepper. Roast for 20 minutes, until al dente. You can be cooking the other ingredients while the cauliflower is roasting, but keep an eye on it to avoid overcooking.

3. In a large pot, heat the grapeseed oil on medium-high. Add the onion and cook until softened, approximately 10 minutes, stirring occasionally. Add the minced garlic and ginger and cook another few minutes. Season with the salt and pepper.

4. Add the cardamom, mustard seeds, and cloves, and cook for 30 seconds, until fragrant.

5. Stir in the turmeric, cumin, rhubarb, and lentils. Add the stock and bring to a boil. Reduce the heat and cover. Simmer for another 20 minutes, stirring occasionally.

6. Stir in the roasted cauliflower and simmer 10 minutes more.

7. Garnish with cilantro, if desired.

Note
• Rhubarb stalks can be cleaned, chopped into 1-inch chunks, and frozen raw for use in the winter months.
• If rhubarb isn't available, 3 cups chopped and peeled green apples are a delicious substitute.

Polenta Greens Casserole

An excellent dish for a crowd, this recipe uses a number of ingredients that need to be prepared in advance. Even if you substitute some store-bought equivalents, you'll have quite a satisfying entrée that requires only a green salad and some good bread to round out the meal.

Serves 10 in a 15- x 10- x 1.5-inch baking dish, or your favorite lasagna pan

Prepare in advance

Roasted Red Peppers, page 242
or Oven-Dried Tomatoes, page 243

Nutty Parm, page 241

Basil Pesto, page 232

Artisanal Ricotta cheese, page 18

Marinara Sauce, page 231

Ingredients

1 (24-ounce) bag finely ground polenta (see notes)

¾ cup Nutty Parm

½ cup basil pesto

salt and freshly ground pepper to taste

2 bunches of mixed greens, coarsely chopped (spinach, Swiss chard, kale, or whatever you like)

olive oil

3 roasted red peppers
or 1 cup oven-dried tomatoes

1 pound crimini or shiitake mushrooms, sliced

4 to 5 cloves garlic, chopped

2 cups Artisanal Ricotta Cheese

2 cups marinara sauce

Method

1. Cook the polenta according to package directions.

2. When the polenta is done, stir in ¼ cup of the Nutty Parm, the pesto, and salt and pepper to taste.

3. Preheat the oven to 350 degrees.

4. Spread the polenta in a casserole dish oiled with cooking spray.

5. In a large skillet, sauté the greens in some olive oil until wilted. Stir in the roasted red peppers or oven-dried tomatoes, add salt and pepper to taste, cook briefly, and transfer to a bowl.

6. In the same skillet, sauté the mushrooms in the olive oil (add more if needed) on medium heat. When the mushrooms begin to soften, add the garlic and continue to sauté until the mushrooms are browned. Set aside when done.

7. On top of the polenta in the casserole dish, add a layer of the greens, then ricotta, then mushrooms. Drizzle marinara sauce on top and sprinkle with the remaining ½ cup Nutty Parm.

8. Bake for 45 minutes.

9. Serve with extra marinara sauce on the side.

Note
• The fine polenta makes for a creamier casserole than the medium grind.
• To prepare in advance: Assemble the casserole, cover tightly, and refrigerate. Bring to room temperature before baking.
• This freezes well. You can make two smaller casseroles and freeze one (baked or unbaked), if you like.

Patty's Potato-Kale Mash

Please take our word for it and just try this dish. It's always greeted by a crescendo of excited "Oooohs" every time it is served at the Spiral House, where it is one of Patty's favorites. To bring some protein into the meal, we generally add garbanzos or nuts to our side salad. This is comfort food to the tenth power.

Serves 6

Prepare in advance

Mushroom Gravy, page 234

Ingredients

3 pounds Yukon gold potatoes (peeled) or red skin potatoes (unpeeled), cut into equal-size chunks

2 tablespoons olive oil

4 tablespoons Earth Balance Vegan Buttery Stick

1 large onion, diced

3 large cloves garlic, chopped

2 to 3 large bunches of kale, stems removed, leaves coarsely chopped

1 pound carrots, peeled and shredded

½ cup soy creamer

salt and freshly ground pepper to taste

1 teaspoon dried thyme

2 tablespoons Bragg Liquid Aminos

vegetable stock or potato cooking water as needed

2 cups mushroom gravy

Note
• As a variation, mix mashed sweet potato with the mashed white potato.

Method

1. In a large pot, combine the potatoes with enough water to cover, bring to a boil. Add salt and cook until fork-tender.

2. While the potatoes cook, use a large sauté pan to heat the olive oil and 2 tablespoons of Earth Balance. Sauté the onions and garlic until translucent.

3. Add the kale to the sauté pan and cook until it starts to wilt, approximately 5 minutes, stirring occasionally.

4. Add the shredded carrots and cook a few minutes longer until carrots soften. Turn off the heat and cover the pan to keep the kale warm.

5. When the potatoes are done, drain them, saving 2 cups of the cooking water if you plan to make our Mushroom Gravy recipe.

6. Mash the potatoes, adding the remaining 2 table-spoons of Earth Balance, the soy creamer, and salt and pepper to taste.

7. Fold the mashed potatoes into the kale mixture in the pan and stir to combine.

8. Add the thyme, Bragg, salt and pepper to taste, and some vegetable stock if the mixture is dry.

9. Whether serving as individual portions or from a large serving bowl, make a well in the potato-kale mash and add some warm mushroom gravy. Serve the remainder of the gravy in a bowl or gravy boat on the table.

Anytime Chili

People can be fiercely opinionated about how to make chili. We like ours with chocolate and coffee added to the already complex balance of flavors. And of course a slice of corn bread (page 189) on the side.

Serves 6 to 8

Prepare in advance

4 cups home-cooked beans, if not using canned beans

Ingredients

5 tablespoons olive oil

5 medium-size onions, chopped

5 cloves garlic, finely chopped

2 red bell peppers, chopped

1 green bell pepper, chopped

2 large or 3 medium zucchini, cubed

1 (28-ounce) can of crushed tomatoes

4 cups black beans (home-cooked or canned, your preference) or a mix of whichever beans you like

2 tablespoons ground cumin

3 tablespoons chili powder or a mix of ancho, chipotle, and chili powders

salt and freshly ground pepper to taste

1 tablespoon unsweetened cocoa powder

½ cup brewed coffee (can be leftover coffee)

2 tablespoons maple syrup

¼ to ½ cup chopped fresh cilantro, chopped

cilantro sprigs, for garnish (optional)

Method

1. In a large pot, heat the olive oil and sauté the onions and garlic until tender.

2. Add the red and green peppers and the zucchini and cook a few more minutes.

3. Stir in the tomatoes with their juices, beans, cumin, chili powder, and salt and pepper to taste. Cook for 15 minutes.

4. Stir in the cocoa powder, coffee, and maple syrup.

5. Simmer for 30 minutes to allow time for the flavors to meld. Stir in cilantro and adjust seasoning to taste. Just before serving, garnish with cilantro sprigs, if you like.

Note
• Freezes well.

Wild Mushroom Stroganoff

Our version of this traditional Russian dish doesn't take much time at all to prepare and if the noodles are gluten-free, then so is your entrée. It's attractive, nourishing, and satisfying fare whether you are serving company or not, and a good way to try Beyond Chicken Strips (see page 267 in Kitchen Wisdom) as an alternative to tofu.

Serves 4

Ingredients

1½ tablespoons Earth Balance Vegan Buttery Stick

1 cup sliced shiitake mushroom caps

1 cup sliced oyster mushrooms, hard stems removed

2 tablespoons olive oil

2 medium-size onions, sliced

2 shallots, sliced

1 large leek, roots and tough green outer part removed, remainder cut in half lengthwise, sliced thin, and rinsed well

2 teaspoons sweet paprika

1 teaspoon smoked paprika

½ teaspoon salt

½ teaspoon ground white pepper

1 tablespoon fresh thyme

⅓ cup Madeira wine

½ cup red wine

1 pound noodles of your choice

½ cup cold water

1 tablespoon cornstarch

1 (12-ounce) container vegan sour cream

½ cup vegetable stock

1 (12-ounce) package Beyond Chicken Grilled Strips or extra-firm tofu

chopped flat-leaf parsley, for garnish

Method

1. Put a large pot of water on to boil for cooking the noodles.

2. Melt the Earth Balance in a sauté pan over medium heat. Add the shiitake and oyster mushrooms and cook until they brown, stirring just enough to keep them from burning. Transfer the mushrooms to a bowl and set aside.

3. In the same pan, heat the olive oil on low heat. Add the onions, shallots, leek, both paprikas, the salt and pepper and sauté until the vegetables are soft.

4. Returning the mushrooms to the pan, add the thyme, Madeira, and red wine. Stir lightly and simmer for approximately 15 minutes to combine all the flavors.

5. While the mushrooms and seasonings are simmering, cook your pasta according to the package directions, being careful to watch that it doesn't overcook while you finish preparing the sauce.

6. Shake the cold water and cornstarch together in a jar to make a slurry. Drizzle it slowly into the mushroom mixture while stirring. The sauce will thicken at this point.

7. Stir in the sour cream and stock, add the chicken-free strips, and stir again. Simmer for a few minutes to combine the flavors.

8. Serve the stroganoff over the noodles and garnish with chopped parsley.

Spanakopycat

This has all the same ingredients as the classic Greek spanakopita, just veganized and served as an easy-to-prepare casserole. Add one of our salads and you have the perfect dinner for eight.

Serves 8

Prepare in advance

Artisanal Ricotta Cheese, page 18

Ingredients

3 tablespoons Earth Balance Vegan Buttery Stick plus 1 stick

1 onion, diced

3 cloves garlic, chopped

2 pounds fresh spinach, chopped

salt and freshly ground pepper to taste

2 cups Artisanal Ricotta Cheese

1 (16-ounce) box filo dough, defrosted

½ cup bread crumbs

2 tablespoons toasted sesame seeds

Note
• The night before you plan to make this casserole, put the box of frozen filo in the refrigerator to defrost overnight.
• To prepare this dish in advance: In step 8, coat the top layer of filo really well with melted Earth Balance and cover tightly before refrigerating. Bring to room temperature before baking.
• To make as an appetizer, prepare the spinach filling as described in steps 1 to 4, then follow the folding method for Filo Reubens, page 23.

Method

1. In a large skillet, heat 3 tablespoons of the Earth Balance, add the onion and garlic, and sauté until softened.

2. Add the spinach, season with salt and pepper, and sauté quickly.

3. Drain the spinach in a colander or on a clean dish towel set on a baking sheet.

4. Put the spinach mixture in a bowl. Add the Artisanal Ricotta Cheese and mix well.

5. Preheat the oven to 350 degrees.

6. Melt the remaining stick Earth Balance and brush the bottom and sides of a 9- x 13-inch casserole. Carefully unfold a sheet of filo, place it on the bottom of the casserole, and brush the sheet with melted Earth Balance. Continue layering and brushing filo, and sprinkling bread crumbs between each layer, until you have 3 sheets of filo.

7. Spread half the spinach mixture on top, then continue layering another stack of 3 filo sheets, brushing liberally with Earth Balance and adding bread crumbs between each layer.

8. Spread the remaining spinach mixture on top, and finish by layering 3 more filo sheets as described in step 6.

9. Sprinkle the top with toasted sesame seeds.

10. Bake uncovered for approximately 45 minutes, or until lightly browned.

Squash Puttanesca

...e cooked flesh of this canary-yellow gourd was all the rage because of ...long strands that could be twirled around a fork and which did, indeed, ...still like spaghetti squash but think it requires a flavorful companion like ...uce, our pairing here.

Serves 4

Prepare in advance

Basil Pesto, page 232

Oven-Dried Tomatoes, page 243

Rafferty's Puttanesca Sauce, page 229

Ingredients

1 large spaghetti squash

4 cloves garlic, chopped

2 tablespoons olive oil

½ cup Kalamata olives, plus a little of the liquid from the olive container

½ cup basil pesto

1 cup oven-dried cherry or grape tomatoes

¼ cup capers, drained

2 cups Rafferty's Puttanesca Sauce

Method

1. Poke the squash with a fork a few times, then cook whole in boiling water for 45 minutes or until fork-tender. You may also oven-roast the squash whole (be sure to pierce with a fork in several places if roasting).

2. On a baking sheet, split the squash in half and let cool, then remove the seeds. Using a large fork, scrape the spaghetti-like squash ribbons away from the skin; set aside.

3. In a large pan, sauté the garlic in olive oil. Then, one at a time, add olives, pesto, dried tomatoes, and capers, giving a quick stir and heating each ingredient before adding the next.

4. Mix the spaghetti squash into the sautéed vegetables and heat through.

5. Serve the squash spaghetti topped with warmed Puttanesca Sauce.

...ttage Pie

...thday lunch every year and, since it's a crew favorite, we have it on ...virtual meal in a single casserole, this dish refrigerates and freezes well, ...f which makes it a good choice to take to a potluck . . . or not take ...njoy at home.

Serves 12 for lunch, 8 for dinner

Prepare in advance

1 firm (14-ounce) tofu cake, frozen, thawed, and pressed to remove excess moisture; cut into small cubes

2 (9-inch) prebaked piecrusts, sugar omitted, pages 248 and 249 (optional)

3 cups mashed potatoes (use white or sweet potatoes, or a combination); can add parsley and minced garlic

Ingredients

1 cup peeled and chopped carrots

2 cups chopped broccoli

6 tablespoons Earth Balance Vegan Buttery Stick

2 medium-size onions, diced

2 large cloves garlic, finely chopped

1 pound mushrooms, chopped

1 firm tofu cake

½ cup toasted walnuts, chopped

6 tablespoons all-purpose flour

½ cup chopped flat-leaf parsley

½ teaspoon fresh thyme

salt and freshly ground pepper to taste

½ cup white wine

3 tablespoons tamari

1 cup vegetable or mushroom broth

½ cup soy creamer

2 cups frozen peas, defrosted

juice of ½ lemon

2 (9-inch) unsweetened piecrusts (optional)

10 white potatoes, sweet potatoes, or a combination

Method

1. Preheat the oven to 400 degrees.

2. Blanch the carrots in boiling salted water until al dente. Remove with a slotted spoon.

3. In the same cooking water, blanch the broccoli, then drain and set aside with the carrots.

4. Melt the Earth Balance in a large pan and sauté the onions and garlic.

5. Add the mushrooms and prepared tofu, and cook until the mushrooms are soft and tofu is browned.

6. Stir in the walnuts, flour, parsley, and thyme and season with salt and pepper.

7. Add the wine, tamari, broth, and soy creamer. Cook for 5 to 8 minutes, until the liquid has reduced and the sauce thickens. Remove from heat.

8. Stir in the blanched carrots and broccoli, the peas, and then the lemon juice.

9. Pour into the prebaked pie shells or, the way most of us prefer, directly into a greased baking dish.

10. Top with mashed potatoes. To create an irregular texture on top, use the back of a spoon to scruff up the potatoes.

11. Bake for 30 to 35 minutes or until golden brown. Baking time may vary depending on the size of the pan or casserole.

Note
• Refrigerates well.
• Freezes well.
• This dish reheats beautifully.
• Freezing the tofu in advance, as described, keeps it from becoming soggy or chewy.

Sides

Birdhouse
Sculpture by Tom Gottsleben,
bluestone, stainless steel, redwood or cedar,
copper, and aluminum with concrete base

(above) *Your Love Is Like a Rainbow*, along the drive up to the Spiral House.
Sculpture by Tom Gottsleben
bluestone, crystal glass, stainless steel, aluminum, concrete, glass aggregate

Rainbow Grilled Vegetables

The outdoor grill and picnic table are within view of Tom's rainbow sculpture. Here and elsewhere on the property, the sun dances with the crystal glass in the sculpture, throwing patches of the color spectrum on the building facade, the stone terraces and pathways, and even on the people passing by. So when we see a colorful array of vegetables, it's an easy leap to name it for the rainbow.

For the vegetables

Vegetables of your choice, such as: portobello mushrooms, asparagus, flat Italian green beans, zucchini, baby bok choy, radicchio, baby onions, baby carrots (see notes)

grapeseed oil, for drizzling

For the rub

1½ tablespoons granulated garlic

1 tablespoon dried oregano

1 tablespoon dried basil

1 teaspoon salt

1 teaspoon freshly ground pepper

½ teaspoon smoky paprika

1 teaspoon ground cumin

Note
• Some root vegetables like parsnips and larger carrots should be parboiled before grilling.
• As an alternative to grilling, you can roast the vegetables in a preheated 425-degree oven until tender. When roasting, use a baking sheet lined with parchment paper. And arrange the vegetables in a single layer to ensure that they roast rather than steam.

Method

1. Mix together the rub ingredients and sprinkle over the vegetables. Drizzle with grapeseed oil and toss.

2. Place the veggies on a hot grill or grill pan, cook until tender turning only once. If you turn repeatedly, the vegetables will get mushy.

Autumn Root Cake

As those fall breezes begin to whip about, here's a harvest-time recipe that's perfect for Thanksgiving, or as the accompaniment to any entrée during the colder months. Try placing each portion on a grilled portobello mushroom and you'll triple the "Wow!" factor.

Serves 6

Ingredients

1 small rutabaga, peeled and cubed

1 celeriac, peeled and cubed

4 medium-size russet potatoes, peeled and cubed

1 large sweet potato

2 leeks, roots trimmed off, dark woody outer leaves discarded

3 tablespoons olive oil

4 tablespoons Earth Balance Vegan Buttery Stick

2 large cloves garlic, chopped

2 large shallots, thinly sliced

salt and freshly ground pepper to taste

2 tablespoons chopped flat-leaf parsley

2 tablespoons fresh dill

1 tablespoon Bragg Liquid Aminos

pinch of ground nutmeg

Method

1. Place the rutabaga, celeriac, and potatoes in separate pots of cold water and bring to a boil. Add salt to the water and cook until tender. The three vegetables have different cooking times; as each one is done, drain and transfer them to a single large bowl.

2. While the vegetables cook, use a fork to pierce the sweet potato in several places. Place it directly on the oven rack with a baking sheet on the rack below, and bake in a preheated 400-degree oven for 1 hour or until tender.

3. While the sweet potato bakes, thinly slice the leeks and clean them by swishing them in a bowl of cold water and letting the dirt sink to the bottom. Remove leek slices with a slotted spoon and set them aside.

4. Heat the olive oil and Earth Balance together in a pan and sauté the garlic, shallots, and leek until tender. Remove from the pan and set aside.

5. Peel the baked sweet potato and add it to the bowl with the rutabaga, celeriac, and white potatoes. Mash everything together.

6. Season the mashed root vegetables with salt and pepper to taste, along with the parsley and dill. Stir in the leek, garlic, and shallot mixture. Add the Bragg and nutmeg, then stir.

7. Scoop up approximately ¼ cup of the mashed vegetables and shape into a patty (or use a pastry bag with a wide tip). Place the patty on a parchment-lined baking sheet sprayed with oil. Repeat.

8. Bake in a 350-degree oven for 20 to 25 minutes.

Braised Fennel with Saffron

This anise-flavored member of the parsley family is widely available from autumn through early spring. A key ingredient in Mediterranean cuisine, it has a crunchy, slightly sweet flavor that is wonderful in winter salads. Here we have fennel simmering in sauce, which makes for a satisfying and substantial vegetable.

Serves 6

Prepare in advance

Roasted Vegetable Stock, page 246

Ingredients

6 large fennel bulbs

6 cloves garlic, chopped

6 large shallots, sliced (about 1 cup)

3 tablespoons olive oil

¼ cup capers, drained

2 sprigs fresh thyme

1 teaspoon red pepper flakes

5 pinches saffron

½ cup vegetable stock

2 (28-ounce) cans San Marzano crushed tomatoes

½ cup white wine

Note
• To enhance the flavor of the sauce, add your fennel trimmings to whatever stock you are using and let it simmer while you prepare the fennel.

Method

1. Trim off the tops and base of the fennel bulbs and quarter the bulbs lengthwise. Take care to leave some part of the core intact on each piece so they will hold their shape during cooking.

2. On medium-high heat, sauté the fennel, garlic, and shallots in olive oil until slightly tender and golden brown, 15 to 20 minutes. Stir in the capers, thyme, and red pepper flakes.

3. Dissolve the saffron in hot stock, then add it to the sauté pan along with the tomatoes. Add the white wine. Reduce the heat to medium-low, cover the pan, and braise until tender, 20 to 25 minutes.

4. Remove thyme sprigs before serving.

Speedy Sautéed Watermelon Radishes

You might walk right past these in the market without having any idea of the beautiful color and pattern inside. Unlike the more common red-skin radish, which gets increasingly pungent as it gets larger, this heirloom gets sweeter. A cool-season crop, watermelon radishes are generally available in spring or late fall and are sure to be a standout on any table.

Serves 2

Ingredients

4 tablespoons Earth Balance Vegan Buttery Stick

1 bunch of watermelon radishes, thinly sliced

salt and freshly ground pepper

Method

1. In a sauté pan on high heat, melt the Earth Balance, then add radishes.

2. Reduce the heat, cover the pan, and simmer for 3 to 4 minutes until tender.

3. Season with salt and pepper to taste.

Oven-Roasted Asparagus

Forget blanching or steaming asparagus (unless you are using them for a salad). Pan-roasting is easier and concentrates the flavor. We also like asparagus cooked on a grill outside.

Serves 6

Ingredients

2 bunches of asparagus

2 tablespoons olive oil

salt and freshly ground pepper

2 teaspoons fresh thyme

zest of 1 lemon

Note
• Don't use lemon juice or the asparagus will become discolored.

Method

1. Preheat the oven to 425 degrees.

2. Cut off the tough ends of asparagus. Peel the bottom half of stalks, if desired.

3. Coat the asparagus with olive oil and sprinkle with salt, pepper, and thyme

4. Arrange in a single layer on a baking sheet lined with parchment paper. Roast for 20 minutes or until tender, shaking the pan once or twice to keep the asparagus from burning.

5. Sprinkle with lemon zest and serve.

Ronnie's Favorite String Beans

Ronnie Shushan, the designer of this cookbook and a writer who is working on a book about the creation of the Spiral House, gave us this recipe because we share her love of garlic. A staple of both the kitchen pantry and the herbal medicine chest, garlic is reputed to contain a little bit of just about everything our bodies require. Long, slow cooking — in the skillet here or oven-roasted — mellows garlic's pungency and gives it a creaminess that makes it spread divinely on a good bread.

Serves 4 for each pound of string beans

Ingredients

8 cloves garlic, peeled (at least 2 cloves per serving, more if you are a garlic lover)

extra-virgin olive oil

1 pound green beans, blanched or not, depending on size and personal preference

coarse salt

½ cup chopped flat-leaf parsley, or more if you like

crusty bread (optional)

Note
• We like to use wide Italian-style green beans in this dish.

Method

1. Sauté the garlic cloves in olive oil over very low heat until they are soft all the way through and a little browned but not burned. Be patient, stir often, and keep an eye on the pan.

2. When the garlic is lightly brown and tender, remove with a slotted spoon and set aside for finishing.

3. Add the beans to the garlicky olive oil and cook over high heat until tender-crisp. It's fine if some of them are a little blackened.

4. Season with a good coarse salt.

5. Toward the end of cooking, add the chopped parsley, and return the garlic to the pan for a quick stir.

6. Serve with a good crusty bread.

Sautéed Greens with Herbs

A Deborah Madison–inspired recipe, this has become a staple at the Spiral House. You can vary it endlessly depending on your taste in greens; we lean toward the robust and spicier greens in general, and particularly in this dish where they hold their own with the strong flavors of the garlic, cumin, and cilantro.

Serves 4

Ingredients

1 pound assorted greens, roughly chopped separately (we use Swiss chard, kale, mustard greens, and sorrel)

5 tablespoons olive oil

4 cloves garlic

1 teaspoon salt

2 handfuls each of fresh basil, parsley, and cilantro

1 teaspoon smoked paprika

2 teaspoons ground cumin

1 lemon, cut into wedges

Method

1. Wash the greens, removing strings and tough stalks.

2. Heat 2 tablespoons of the olive oil in a large sauté pan. Sauté the tougher greens first, then the more tender ones, and cook until all the greens are tender. Transfer to a bowl and set aside.

3. Using a mortar and pestle, mash the garlic and salt together, then add the herbs and pound everything together into a rough paste. You can make the paste in a food processor, but we really do prefer this one done by hand; you'll see it's not much more work.

4. Using the same pan, slowly warm the remaining 3 tablespoons of olive oil with the paprika and cumin. Add the garlic-herb paste and stir to combine. Return the greens to the pan, toss everything together, and cook for 1 to 2 minutes more.

5. Transfer to a serving bowl and garnish with the lemon wedges.

Whistle Stop Fried Green Tomatoes

Fried green tomatoes leapt out of Southern cuisine and into ordinary American kitchens in the late 1980s with the publication of *Fried Green Tomatoes at the Whistle Stop Café*, a novel by Fannie Flagg and later a movie. Weaving together stories across generations, its themes exemplify much of what is important to us here at the Spiral House: good friends, good food, and good will.

Serves 4

Prepare in advance

Creamy Citrus-Chive Dipping Sauce, page 224

2 cups cashews soaked in warm water for 2 hours

Seasoning mix

1 teaspoon Cajun seasoning

1 teaspoon chili powder

1 teaspoon smoked paprika

1 teaspoon onion powder

1 teaspoon granulated garlic

salt and freshly ground pepper

Ingredients

2 cups raw cashews

½ cup rice flour

½ cup fine-grind cornmeal

3 to 4 unripened green tomatoes

sea salt

2 flax eggs (1 flax egg = 1 tablespoon flaxseed soaked in 3 tablespoons warm water for 5 minutes)

4 tablespoons Earth Balance shortening or grapeseed oil, for frying, more if needed

Method

1. Drain cashews and blend in a food processor with ¾ cup of water to make a thick creamy batter.

2. Stir together the seasoning mix ingredients and divide between two bowls. Mix the flour into one bowl; mix the cornmeal into the other bowl.

3. Cut the tomatoes into ½-inch-thick slices, sprinkle with sea salt, and set aside for 5 minutes.

4. In a shallow dish, mix together the creamed cashews and the flax eggs.

5. In a large frying pan, melt the shortening over medium-high heat. You should have approximately ½ inch oil for frying.

6. Arrange the three bowls (seasoned flour, cashew mixture, and seasoned cornmeal) in a line. Dredge the tomato slices first in the flour mixture, shaking off the excess; then in the cashew mixture, moistening both sides; then in the cornmeal.

7. Drop the tomato slices carefully into the hot oil and fry until lightly browned, approximately 4 minutes. Do not crowd the pan. Turn and fry on the other side until lightly browned, only a few minutes more. Let rest on a wire cooling rack placed over a baking sheet. Blot gently with a paper towel to remove excess oil.

8. Serve hot with citrus-chive dipping sauce.

Note
• Pepper jelly is another good condiment here.

Crispy Potato Fans

This impressive-looking side dish is not much more difficult to make than your average baked spud. These have a yin-yang appeal, combining the crispiness of French fries with the creaminess of a well-baked potato. Some of us think they are perfect with just a little extra salt and pepper; others like to add an extra step, stuffing them with a non-dairy cheese or sauce. And we all wonder why none of us ever had them before.

Serves 6

Ingredients

6 Idaho or russet potatoes, peeled

1 cup olive oil

salt and freshly ground pepper to taste

1 teaspoon chopped fresh rosemary

1 teaspoon chopped fresh thyme

6 cloves garlic, chopped (or 1 clove per potato, if you are making more or less than the recipe suggests)

Note
• Diane uses Idaho or russet potatoes here because they hold up great and have a distinctive oval shape that makes an attractive presentation

Method

1. Preheat the oven to 375 degrees.

2. Cut a small slice from the bottom of each potato so it sits flat.

3. Working from one end of the potato to the other, cut thin slits, slicing almost to the bottom but not completely through. These cuts need not be wide; the potatoes will fan out as they bake. Immediately place the potatoes in cold water after slicing to keep them from discoloring.

4. In a shallow bowl, mix the olive oil, salt and pepper, rosemary, thyme, and garlic. Drain and dry the potatoes, then roll the potatoes one at a time in the olive oil mixture to coat.

5. Arrange the potatoes in a baking dish and pour any excess seasoned oil over them.

6. Bake for 45 to 60 minutes, or until crispy and brown on top.

Smashed Potatoes

Easy as can be, these potatoes bring comfort food to new heights. They really are smashed, exposing a lot of surface area to absorb the seasonings as they bake the second time around. No matter how many potatoes come out of the oven, the platter is always laid bare.

Serves 8

Prepare in advance

Nutty Parm, page 241

For the potatoes

8 red skin or new potatoes, skins on

¼ cup rub (recipe follows)

1 Earth Balance Vegan Buttery Stick

Nutty Parm, for sprinkling

For the rub

Makes ¼ cup

leaves from 4 sprigs of rosemary, chopped

leaves from 4 sprigs thyme, chopped

2 tablespoons chopped fresh flat-leaf parsley

zest of 2 lemons

¼ cup minced garlic

salt and freshly ground pepper to taste

Method

1. Preheat the oven to 375 degrees.

2. Mix together the rub ingredients in a small bowl. Set aside.

3. Pierce the potatoes with a fork and bake directly on the oven rack until almost soft, 30 to 40 minutes.

4. Put the potatoes in a baking dish and smash them with a large spoon.

5. Sprinkle the rub on top of the potatoes and top each with a pat of Earth Balance and a sprinkling of Nutty Parm.

6. Return the potatoes to the oven and bake until done, approximately 20 minutes.

Note
• You can bake the potatoes and refrigerate them overnight. When ready to serve: smash, season, and finish baking them in a preheated oven.

Good Baked Potatoes

...ıgredient for any twice-baked potato. So gather your favorite ingredients
... of itself, and rightly so. Here, Chef Diane chose to add her Nutty Parm and
..., two favorites among our group. We try to make extra for freezing, but
... left over to actually make it to the freezer.

Serves 12

Prepare in advance

Nutty Parm, page 241

Oven-Dried Tomatoes, page 243
(optional)

Ingredients

6 large baking potatoes (½ potato per person), scrubbed

2 bunches of broccoli, chopped after removing the woody stems

2 tablespoons olive oil

1 large yellow onion, finely chopped

4 cloves garlic, finely chopped

2 cups sliced mushrooms

4 tablespoons Earth Balance Vegan Buttery Stick, at room temperature

½ cup chopped fresh flat-leaf parsley

¾ cup vegan sour cream

salt and freshly ground pepper to taste

Nutty Parm, for sprinkling

oven-dried tomatoes (optional)

Method

1. Preheat the oven to 400 degrees.

2. Prick the potatoes all over with a fork and bake until fork-tender.

3. While the potatoes bake, blanch the broccoli, drain well, and set aside.

4. Heat the olive oil in a large sauté pan. Sauté the onions, garlic, and mushrooms until lightly browned.

5. Reduce the oven temperature to 350 degrees.

6. When the potatoes are done, split each one in half lengthwise. Carefully scoop out the potato into a large bowl, being careful not to tear the skins.

7. Mash the potatoes and mix in the blanched broccoli, onion-mushroom mixture, Earth Balance, parsley, and sour cream. Season with salt and pepper.

8. Fill the potato skins with the potato mixture.

9. Top with Nutty Parm and Oven-Dried Tomatoes, if desired.

10. Bake for 20 to 25 minutes, until heated through and lightly browned on top.

Note
• Freezes well, baked or unbaked.

Smoky Baked Beans with "Chorizo"

It may look like a lot of steps, but you can soak the beans during the day and bake the dish for dinner with relatively little effort. Good old American baked beans are believed to have been inspired by the French cassoulets and English stews that sailors brought to America hundreds of years ago. But Chef Diane has definitely added her own signature with the smoky flavor and plant-based "chorizo" featured in her version. It's a staple dish at the Spiral House.

Makes about 13 cups

Prepare in advance

1 pound dried mixed beans (we use pintos and butter beans), washed and soaked for 8 hours

Ingredients

¼ cup olive oil

8 ounces plant-based chorizo (see note), removed from casing and crumbled

4 cups chopped white onions

8 cloves garlic, thinly sliced

1 pound presoaked mixed dried beans (see note)

6 cups water

2 tablespoons chopped fresh oregano

2 tablespoons chopped fresh thyme

1 tablespoon salt, or to taste

1 teaspoon ground cumin

½ teaspoon smoked paprika

½ teaspoon paprika

2 bay leaves

2 tablespoons brown sugar

3 tablespoons molasses

½ cup ketchup

¼ teaspoon red pepper flakes

2½ tablespoons red wine vinegar

¼ teaspoon freshly ground pepper

⅛ teaspoon ground white pepper

½ cup chopped scallions

2 tablespoons chopped flat-leaf parsley

Method

1. Heat the olive oil in a large Dutch oven or any heavy pot (preferably cast iron) over medium heat. Add the chorizo and sauté for about 4 minutes.

2. Add the onions and garlic and sauté for another 8 to 10 minutes or until onions are soft.

3. Add the beans and water to the pot, along with the oregano, thyme, salt, cumin, both paprikas, and bay leaves. Bring to a boil, cover, and reduce the heat. Simmer for 45 minutes or until the beans are just tender.

4. Preheat the oven to 350 degrees.

5. Stir the sugar, molasses, ketchup, and red pepper flakes into the bean mixture. Cover and transfer to the oven. Bake for 1½ hours or until the beans are very tender and sauce is thick.

6. Remove from the oven and stir in the vinegar, black pepper, and ground white pepper. Discard the bay leaves.

7. Garnish with scallions and parsley before serving.

Note
• Diane uses Trader Joe's Soy Chorizo, which has a good texture and is both delicious and gluten-free.
• When cooking different varieties of beans together, choose ones approximately the same size so they will cook in about the same amount of time.

Chickpea Fries

Known as *panelle* in Sicily, where they are sold as a popular street food, and chickpea fries in vegan jargon, these are made from a thick porridge of chickpea flour that is cooled, cut into shapes, and fried. Flavor them in a dozen different ways and serve with your favorite sauce.

Makes 32 strips

Ingredients

grapeseed oil, for greasing

4 cups water

1 teaspoon granulated garlic

2 cups chickpea flour

2 teaspoons salt, plus more for sprinkling

½ teaspoon freshly ground pepper, plus more for sprinkling

¼ cup olive oil

grapeseed oil, for frying

2 lemons, cut into wedges

Note
• Allow time for the chickpea mixture to chill before frying.

Method

1. Oil a baking sheet and line it with parchment paper. Oil the paper.

2. In a saucepan, bring the water to a boil. Add the granulated garlic and gradually add the chickpea flour, whisking rapidly to prevent lumps.

3. Season with salt and pepper, then reduce the heat to a simmer. Check seasoning.

4. Stir in the olive oil and cook for a minute, until the chickpea mixture forms a thick porridge.

5. Scoop the chickpea mixture onto the parchment paper and spread it into an even layer. Let it cool and then cover loosely with parchment paper or plastic wrap.

6. Chill for 1 hour in the refrigerator or 30 minutes in the freezer, until the chickpea porridge is firm to the touch.

7. When cooled, lift the parchment paper, flip chilled chickpea mixture over onto a cutting board, and cut into French fry shapes about 3 inches long.

8. Heat at least ¼ inch of grapeseed oil in a large skillet over medium heat. It is hot enough when the oil bubbles around a wooden spoon.

9. Using tongs and working in batches, gently drop the fries into the hot oil, rotating them occasionally until they are golden all over, for 3 to 4 minutes.

10. Use a large slotted spoon to remove the fries to a wire cooling rack. Blot the top with paper towels. Immediately sprinkle with salt and a lot of pepper. Serve hot with lemon wedges on the side.

Irish Eyes Soda Bread

Who would think you could make an Irish Soda bread without buttermilk? Actually, buttermilk is easy to veganize with the same workaround used by any savvy cook caught without buttermilk: Add some apple cider vinegar or lemon juice to whatever plant-based milk you have on hand. When this bread came out of the oven, the kitchen crew huddled around the butcher's block as a crescendo of voices sought to convince Diane that the bread didn't need to be cooled before slicing. Feel free to serve warm, or at room temperature if you can wait.

Serves 6 to 8

Ingredients

1½ cups non-dairy milk

2 teaspoons apple cider vinegar or lemon juice

4 cups all-purpose flour

2 tablespoons sugar (optional)

2 teaspoons baking soda

1 teaspoon caraway seeds

1 cup dried currants or raisins

1 teaspoon salt

4 tablespoons Earth Balance Vegan Buttery Stick, melted

Note
• This bread makes great toast.

Method

1. Preheat the oven to 350 degrees.

2. Combine the milk with the vinegar or lemon juice and stir to make a plant-based buttermilk.

3. To a large mixing bowl, add the flour, sugar if using, baking soda, caraway seeds, currants or raisins, and salt. Whisk to combine.

4. Slowly mix the buttermilk and 2 tablespoons of melted Earth Balance into the flour mixture, stirring with a wooden spoon until it is slightly sticky. You might not use all the buttermilk; you don't want it as wet as the batter of many quick breads. Don't overmix.

5. Shape the dough into a ball. Don't overwork or it will become tough.

6. Place the dough on a greased baking sheet. Use a serrated knife to score an X at the center of the dough approximately ¼ inch deep.

7. Brush the dough with the remaining 2 tablespoons of melted Earth Balance.

8. Bake for 30 to 45 minutes, until bread is golden and cooked through. Test for doneness by inserting a toothpick. If it comes out clean, it's done. If not, bake for a few minutes more.

9. Let cool slightly before slicing.

Irish Daily Bread

Diane came by this recipe from a friend with Irish roots. Their kids grew up together, and because this bread is so easy to make — really you just stir a few ingredients together and bake — her friend Claire made it all the time. That's one reason they call it Daily Bread. The other reason is that it doesn't keep well, so you should eat it the day it is baked, never a problem around the Spiral House.

Serves 6 to 8

Ingredients

2 tablespoons white or cider vinegar

1 cup non-dairy milk

2 cups whole wheat flour

1 cup all-purpose flour

1½ teaspoons baking soda

1 teaspoon salt

1 Earth Balance Vegan Buttery Stick, melted

Note
• Wonderful paired with soups or stews.

Method

1. Preheat the oven to 350 degrees.

2. In a small bowl, stir the vinegar into the milk to make buttermilk.

3. In a large bowl, whisk together both flours, the baking soda, and salt.

4. Quickly incorporate the buttermilk and melted Earth Balance into the dry ingredients, adding more flour if too wet. Do not overmix.

5. Shape the dough into a ball and place on a greased baking sheet or cast-iron pan. Use a serrated knife to cut an X on top of the dough.

6. Bake for about 45 minutes until brown on top.

7. Let rest for a few minutes before serving.

A-Maizing Corn Bread

With its slightly crunchy texture and melt-in-your-mouth taste, no one would dream this corn bread was made without eggs or dairy. Serve it alongside a bowl of chili, or with maple syrup for a breakfast treat, or just about any time you are craving some quick homemade bread.

Serves 6 to 10

Ingredients

2 tablespoons white vinegar or lemon juice

2 cups soy milk creamer

3 cups finely ground corn meal

1 cup all-purpose flour

3 tablespoons baking powder

1 teaspoon baking soda

1 teaspoon salt

8 ounces non-dairy cream cheese

1 can (11 ounces) corn, or frozen corn, defrosted and drained

4 flax eggs (1 flax egg = 1 tablespoon flaxseed soaked in 3 tablespoons warm water for 5 minutes)

Note
• For crispier crust, preheat your skillet in the oven before filling it with the batter. And for an even moister interior, fill an oven-proof bowl with some water and place it in the oven while the bread bakes.
• Another tip for moist corn bread: Add 1 grated zucchini to your batter.

Method

1. Preheat the oven to 350 degrees.

2. In a small bowl, stir the vinegar or lemon juice into the soy creamer to make buttermilk.

3. Mix all the dry ingredients in one bowl. Mix all the wet ingredients in a second bowl. Add the wet ingredients to the dry ones and stir just until the dry ingredients are moistened.

4. Transfer to a large greased ovenware pan or a 10-inch round cast-iron skillet.

5. Bake for 30 to 40 minutes. Let cool slightly.

Carrot Muffins

Muffins are quick and easy to make, and lend themselves to endless variations. They also freeze well in zip-tight bags, defrost quickly, and are delicious reheated. Here are two of our favorites to add to your repertoire. We often pair them with African Peanut Soup (page 58).

Makes 12 muffins

Ingredients

2 cups kamut flour (see note)

1 cup rolled oats

2 teaspoons baking powder

½ teaspoon salt

2 teaspoons ground cinnamon

½ teaspoon ground nutmeg

½ teaspoon ground ginger

2 cups grated carrots

½ cup coconut oil, liquefied, or canola oil

1 cup unsweetened non-dairy creamer

¾ cup packed brown sugar

2 teaspoons vanilla extract

3 flax eggs (1 flax egg = 1 tablespoon flaxseed soaked in 3 tablespoons warm water for 5 minutes)

Note
• Kamut flour is made from an ancient wheat that is higher in protein and many minerals than modern wheat.

Method

1. Preheat the oven to 375 degrees. Grease a muffin tin, or use baking muffin cups.

2. In a large bowl, whisk together the flour, oats, baking powder, salt, cinnamon, nutmeg, and ginger.

3. Add the carrots and toss with the dry mixture.

4. To another bowl, add the creamer, brown sugar, and vanilla extract. Add the flax eggs and stir.

5. Add the wet ingredients to the dry ingredients, stirring until just combined. Don't overmix.

6. Pour the batter into the greased cups, filling them three-fourths full.

7. Bake the muffins until the tops bounce back when lightly pressed, or when a toothpick inserted in the center comes out clean, 15 to 18 minutes.

8. Remove muffins from the tins and let cool at least 20 minutes before serving.

Zucchini Muffins

Sweetened with applesauce and pumpkin purée, these muffins are another good choice to pair with savory dishes. Don't wait for zucchini season; make them anytime of year.

Makes 12 muffins

Ingredients

6 flax eggs (1 flax egg = 1 tablespoon flaxseed soaked in 3 tablespoons warm water for 5 minutes)

½ cup apple sauce

½ cup pumpkin purée

½ cup grapeseed oil

2 teaspoons vanilla extract

1½ cups whole wheat flour

1½ cups all-purpose flour

1 cup granulated sugar

1 tablespoon baking powder

¾ teaspoon baking soda

2 teaspoons ground cinnamon

1 teaspoon ground nutmeg

1 teaspoon salt

2¼ cups grated zucchini

Method

1. Preheat the oven to 350 degrees.

2. Combine the flax eggs, apple sauce, pumpkin, oil, and vanilla in a medium-size bowl and mix.

3. In a large bowl, mix together both flours, the sugar, baking powder and soda, cinnamon, nutmeg, and salt.

4. Fold the zucchini into the dry ingredients to coat.

5. Add the wet ingredients to the dry ingredients, being careful not to overmix.

6. Grease a muffin tin and pour the batter into the cups, filling them three-fourths full.

7. Bake for 25 to 30 minutes. Let cool and enjoy.

Desserts

Earth Seed (foreground), bluestone,
stainless steel, and crystal glass;
Tangled Up in Blue (middle ground); and
Your Love Is Like a Rainbow (background).
Sculpture by Tom Gottsleben.

Apple Pie

...ple pie? It's so welcoming that it has become synonymous with American ...ane's version up against the winner of any pie contest anywhere. From its ...watering filling, no one would ever suspect that it was made without butter.

Prepare in advance

dough for 2 (9-inch) piecrusts, chilled (for Diane's piecrust dough, see page 248)

Ingredients

9 apples, peeled, cored, and sliced (but not too thinly)

juice of ½ lemon

½ cup granulated sugar

½ cup packed brown sugar, plus extra for sprinkling

2 teaspoons ground cinnamon

½ teaspoon ground nutmeg

2 tablespoons all-purpose flour

dough for 2 (9-inch) piecrusts, chilled

soy creamer, for brushing crust

Method

1. Preheat the oven to 375 degrees.

2. Put the apple slices in a large bowl and sprinkle with the lemon juice. Combine both sugars, the cinnamon, nutmeg, and flour and toss to coat the apple slices.

3. Roll the pie dough into two 12-inch rounds, as described on page 248, steps 4 and 5. Ease one of the rounds of pie dough into the bottom of a pie plate, gently pressing the dough against the sides of the pan. Fill the crust with the apple mixture.

4. Place the top crust over the apple mixture and pinch the top and bottom crusts together. Cut slits in the top of the dough and brush the crust with soy creamer. Sprinkle with brown sugar.

5. Bake for approximately 45 minutes, or until crust is lightly browned. Cool on a wire rack 1 hour to serve warm, or cool completely to serve later.

Note
• Sprinkling lemon juice on the apples will prevent them from turning brown.
• Depending on availability, we use Granny Smiths, Empire, or any other baking apple.

Blueberry Yum Crumble

The combination of cashews, oats, apple cider, and blueberries make this a wholesome dessert you can love. Some of us like to top ours with our favorite plant-based ice cream or gelato. However you serve it, this is a scrumptious dessert for any time that blueberries are available.

Serves 8 to 10

For the crust

2 to 2½ cups toasted cashews

⅓ cup almond butter

1 Earth Balance Vegan Buttery Stick

¼ cup pure maple syrup

½ teaspoon ground cinnamon

¼ cup apple cider

pinch of salt

For the crumble topping

1 Earth Balance Vegan Buttery Stick, at room temperature

1 cup packed brown sugar

1 cup rolled oats

½ cup granulated sugar

½ teaspoon ground nutmeg

1 teaspoon ground cinnamon

For the filling

3½ cups fresh blueberries

1 teaspoon ground cinnamon, or more as needed

1 teaspoon brown sugar, or more as needed

2 tablespoons chestnut flour (or any gluten-free flour)

Method for the crust

1. Preheat the oven to 350 degrees.

2. In a food processor, blend all the crust ingredients until well combined.

3. Press the crust firmly into the bottom and sides of a pie pan.

4. Bake the crust for 20 minutes, or until it is lightly browned.

5. Let cool for a few minutes before filling.

For the crumble topping

Put all the ingredients in a bowl and combine with your fingers.

For the filling

1. While the crust is baking, mix the filling ingredients together. If the blueberries are not sweet, you can add more sugar and cinnamon.

2. Pour the filling into the lightly browned piecrust.

3. Cover with crumble topping.

4. Bake at 350 degrees for 20 minutes or until the filling is bubbly and topping is browned.

5. Let cool before serving.

Note
• Can make ahead.
• Can use crumble topping on any fruit dessert.

Sweet Potato Gingersnap Pie

Here you have our favorite alternative to a traditional pumpkin pie. The sweet potatoes are way less fuss to prepare than a pumpkin, the bourbon adds a bewitching flavor, and the gingersnap crust is deliciously gluten-free. We think it's the perfect pie for the holiday season or any other time you want a scrumptious earthy dessert.

Serves 8

Prepare in advance

Basic Cashew Cream, page 220

For the crust

2 cups gluten-free gingersnaps, crumbled (we use Trader Joe's)

½ cup walnuts, toasted

¼ cup dried apricots, chopped

1 stick Earth Balance Vegan Buttery Stick, melted

For the filling

3 cups cooked, mashed sweet potatoes

¾ cup packed light brown sugar

¾ cup granulated sugar

1¾ teaspoon ground cinnamon

1 teaspoon ground nutmeg

1½ teaspoon ground ginger

⅛ teaspoon ground cloves

3 tablespoons Jack Daniels or other good bourbon

1½ cups Basic Cashew Cream (see notes)

Method for the crust

1. In a food processor, process the gingersnaps until you have fine crumbs.

2. Add toasted walnuts and chopped apricots and process until you have fine crumbs. Add the melted butter and process until combined.

3. Pour the mixture into a 9-inch pie plate and press firmly with your fingers so that the crumbs stick to the bottom and sides of the plate.

4. Cover with plastic wrap and refrigerate for at least 30 minutes.

For the pie filling

1. Preheat the oven to 350 degrees.

2. In a large bowl, combine all the filling ingredients except the cashew cream, and mix to combine. Fold in the cashew cream and pour the filling into the pie shell.

3. Bake for 30 to 40 minutes, or until the center is firm. A toothpick inserted in the center should come out clean when the pie is done.

Note
• Plan ahead: The cashews must be soaked overnight before making the cashew cream.
• You want a thick cashew cream for this recipe.

Mother's Raisin and Date Cake

Chef Diane remembers watching her mother make this cake during the holidays throughout her childhood. "She didn't make it any other time, but from Thanksgiving to Christmas it filled the kitchen with a sweet spicy aroma that I still love," she recalls. "Who knew it would turn out to be vegan? All I had to do was replace conventional shortening with Earth Balance shortening."

Serves 15 to 20

Ingredients

1 cup seedless golden raisins

1 cup dates, chopped

½ cup dried apricots

½ cup dried cherries

1 cup packed light brown sugar

1 cup granulated sugar

2 teaspoons ground cinnamon

1 teaspoon ground nutmeg

½ teaspoon ground cloves

½ teaspoon ground ginger

5 tablespoons Earth Balance Natural Shortening, plus more for greasing the pan

2 cups hot water

2 teaspoons baking soda

3 cups all-purpose flour

1 teaspoon baking powder

1 teaspoon salt

Method

1. In a large pot, combine all the ingredients listed before baking soda. Bring to a full boil, then lower the heat and simmer for 10 minutes, until a syrup forms.

2. In the meantime, preheat the oven to 350 degrees. Generously grease a 10-inch-diameter Bundt-style pan.

3. Remove syrup from the heat and let it cool slightly, for approximately 15 minutes. Stir in the baking soda.

4. Sift together the flour, baking powder, and salt and fold into the pot. Pour the batter into the well-greased Bundt pan.

5. Bake for 1 to 1½ hours, depending on your oven and the size of your Bundt pan. The cake should feel firm to the touch when done. Leave the oven closed until it is time to check for doneness. If you repeatedly open and close the oven door, the cake will sink.

Note
• Stays moist for 10 days without refrigeration — in the unlikely event that it isn't eaten well before then.
• For easy removal of the cake, the pan needs to be well-oiled or greased.

Sweet Rice Timbales

Derived from the French word for "drum," timbales can refer to the kind of pan used for baking or the food that is cooked inside it. Savory or sweet, they can be served as a side, entrée, or dessert. Our sweet recipe is perfect for brunch or as the finish to a light meal. You can shape it using a ring mold, a biscuit cutter, a ramekin, or even a straight-sided measuring cup. The rhubarb sauce is a delicious finale, but you could serve these with any fruit sauce. A delicate touch and a little bit of effort will result in an elegant preparation.

Makes 8 servings

Prepare in advance

Rhubarb Sauce (recipe below) or other fruit sauce

Ingredients

2 cups jasmine rice, uncooked

2 (14-ounce) cans unsweetened coconut milk

1 vanilla bean, split

1 teaspoon salt

½ cup pure maple syrup

1 tablespoon ground cinnamon

½ teaspoon ground nutmeg

1 cup raisins

Method

1. Put the rice, coconut milk, vanilla bean, and salt in a rice cooker or saucepan with a tight lid. Bring to a boil, turn down the heat, cover, and simmer until the rice is tender. (Check package for cook time.)

2. When the rice is done, turn off the heat. Add the maple syrup, cinnamon, nutmeg, and raisins and fluff with a fork to combine.

3. Cover the pot and let the flavors meld for a little while.

4. Spoon the rice mixture into a biscuit cutter (or other mold), and press the rice down firmly into the mold. Slowly lift the cutter straight up. Continue forming the other timbales in this way.

5. Drizzle Rhubarb Sauce over the timbales and each plate, using a plastic squeeze bottle with the tip cut to an appropriately small opening.

Rhubarb Sauce

Because this sauce freezes well, it can top timbales, pound cake, ice cream, and more all year long.

Makes approximately 2 cups

Ingredients

1 pound fresh rhubarb stalks, without leaves (which are toxic)

¾ cup granulated sugar

½ cup orange juice

3 tablespoon cornstarch

1 tablespoon orange liqueur (such as Grand Marnier)

2 tablespoons Earth Balance Vegan Buttery Stick

pinch or two of cinnamon (optional)

½ cup raspberries

½ cup strawberries

Method

1. Rinse the rhubarb stalks, cut off tops and bottoms, and pull away any fibrous strings that run the length of the outside of the stalks. If the stalks are more than half an inch thick, cut them in half length-wise, then cut into 1-inch pieces on the diagonal.

2. Combine the sugar, orange juice, cornstarch, and orange liqueur in a wide, shallow, non-aluminum pan. Add the rhubarb, in a single layer if possible, and bring to a slow boil over low heat, stirring occasionally to dissolve the sugar.

3. Cook for about 15 minutes; remove from heat. Stir in the Earth Balance, and, if you like, cinnamon.

4. Let the sauce cool. Add raspberries and strawberries and blend in a food processor.

Citrus Melon Sorbet

Jane Polcovar, a passionate gardener and member of the kitchen crew, introduced us to this summer cooler that has become a welcome staple in recent years as our Northeast summers get increasingly warm. You don't need an ice cream maker and you can use any combination of fresh fruit to make the sorbet. The better the quality of the fruit, the better the flavor of the sorbet. Here, the star ingredient is cantaloupe and we have paired the sorbet with a strawberry balsamic sauce.

Makes approximately 2 cups

Ingredients

¼ cup orange juice

2 tablespoons lime juice

3 cups cantaloupe chunks

¾ cup sugar

2 teaspoons grated lemon peel

2 teaspoons grated lime peel

Method

1. Combine all the ingredients in a blender jar. Process for 1 to 2 minutes until smooth.

2. Pour the purée into a shallow pan, cover with plastic wrap, and freeze until the edges begin to form ice crystals. Then stir the edges into the middle and return to the freezer.

3. Freeze 2 hours longer or until firm.

4. Just before serving, break into chunks and return to a blender jar. Process for 2 to 3 minutes or until the sorbet is smooth.

Strawberries with Balsamic

The tart vinegar actually enhances the sweetness of the strawberries — such is the alchemy of food combinations. The photo at right shows this sauce paired with our fruit sorbet. It's also wonderful over pound cake and non-dairy ice creams.

Makes 6 servings

Ingredients

3 tablespoons balsamic vinegar

2 tablespoons sugar (if your balsamic vinegar is sweet, omit the sugar)

¼ teaspoon ground black pepper

1 teaspoon vanilla extract (optional)

1 pound fresh strawberries, hulled and halved

Method

1. Combine all the ingredients except the strawberries in a bowl and stir gently.

2. Add the berries to the marinade. Cover and marinate at room temperature for at least 30 minutes. Use within a few hours.

Poached Autumn Pears

There's evidence that we have been eating pears since prehistoric times, although we are pretty certain the fruit consumed by our early ancestors didn't look or taste anything like these Poached Autumn Pears.

Serves 6

Ingredients

2¼ cups apple cider

3¼ cups rosé wine

1 vanilla bean, split in half

1 stick cinnamon, split in half

½ teaspoon ground nutmeg

1 (2-inch) piece of fresh ginger, peeled

1 cup sugar

½ cup pure maple syrup

6 ripe but firm pears (1 pear per person), peeled, stem intact

Method

1. Mix the apple cider, wine, vanilla bean, cinnamon stick, nutmeg, and ginger in a large pot and bring to a simmer.

2. Add the pears, cover the pot, and simmer over medium heat, turning the pears occasionally, until fork-tender.

3. With a slotted spoon, transfer the pears to shallow serving bowls. Add the sugar and maple syrup to the poaching liquid, bring to a boil, then lower the heat to a simmer, stirring occasionally, until the syrup is reduced.

4. Let the syrup cool slightly, then pour it over the poached pears and serve warm.

Broiled Grapefruit

It seems very 1950s, but the sweet-tart flavors of broiled grapefruit make a satisfying end to a rich meal, or a hot breakfast on a cold day. And, hey, mid-century is in.

Serves 4

Ingredients

½ grapefruit per person

pure maple syrup

ground cinnamon, for sprinkling

sprigs of fresh mint (optional)

Method

1. Preheat the broiler.

2. Cut the grapefruit in half crosswise. Using a sharp knife, carefully cut around each segment to loosen the fruit.

3. Place grapefruit halves on a baking sheet. If the halves don't sit upright, cut a thin slice off the bottom of each. Drizzle maple syrup over each half.

3. Broil approximately 10 minutes, until the juices start to bubble and the tops begin to brown.

4. Remove from the oven, sprinkle cinnamon over each half, and garnish with fresh mint if desired.

Andrea's Strudel

Our resident photographer and head gardener (among many other things), Andrea Barrist Stern is passionate about living a vegan lifestyle. She is also passionate about strudel. Of the recipe passed down through her family, she reminisces: "I can hardly remember a holiday or party when either my mother, Edith Barrist, or my Aunt Polly didn't make strudel. My sister-in-law and I have continued that tradition so, today, there is almost no special event in our family or among my friends without it. A vegetarian most of my life, I became a vegan in 2005 and the very first recipe I veganized was strudel. For a long time, no one was the wiser. I simply enjoyed watching everyone savor it, and never said a word." This recipe is way easier than the number of steps might indicate.

Makes approximately 40 pieces

Ingredients

2 Earth Balance Buttery Sticks, cut into small pieces

8 ounces Tofutti cream cheese, at room temperature

2 cups unbleached all-purpose flour, plus more for dusting

3 cups walnuts

ground cinnamon, for sprinkling

about 3 tablespoons sugar

8 ounces golden raisins

2 (13-ounce) jars of your favorite preserves

Tofutti sour cream, at room temperature

Note
• Baked strudel refrigerates for several days, if covered.
• The pastry freezes well in two zip-tight bags, one inside of another or one inside a tightly covered plastic container to prevent freezer burn.

Method

Detailed photos on page 210

1. Put the Earth Balance pieces and cream cheese into a food processor and pulse until they begin to blend.

2. Add 2 tablespoons of the flour to processor and blend, then add the remaining flour. Pulse until a rough ball of dough is formed.

3. Heavily dust your work surface with flour. Shape dough into a smooth ball and cut into 4 equal pieces.

4. Dust each cut edge of dough with flour, and roll each piece into a ball.

5. Wrap the dough balls in plastic wrap and refrigerate for at least 1 hour.

6. In a clean food processor bowl, finely chop the walnuts to a bread crumb consistency.

7. Working with 1 ball of dough at a time, flatten the dough with your palms on a well-floured surface, then roll with a well-floured rolling pin into an oval shape, gently lifting and turning the dough several times and adding more flour to the surface as needed.

8. Continue rolling until you have an approximately 14- x 18-inch shape.

9. Sprinkle generously with cinnamon, about ¾ tablespoon of sugar, 5 heaping tablespoons of nuts, and 3 handfuls of raisins.

10. Drop preserves by the spoonful, about ½ teaspoon at a time.

11. Using a pastry tool as shown in the first photo on page 211, fold the edges of the dough over on all sides. Gently loosen the dough from your surface as you roll lengthwise to the end of the dough.

12. Gently transfer the rolled pastry to a parchment-lined cookie sheet. (See the photo on page 211, bottom left.) Preheat the oven to 400 degrees.

13. Scrape your surface clean, remove the next dough ball from the refrigerator and repeat steps 7 through 12 until you have rolled, shaped, and filled all the dough balls.

14. Spread a thin layer of sour cream over the tops of the rolls.

15. Bake for about 20 minutes, or until the strudel is lightly browned. Cool for 1 hour before cutting.

16. Trim the ends off each roll and discard (or eat). Slice each roll into approximately 10 pieces. Place pieces in decorative foil baking cups.

Andrea Makes Her Strudel

Ingredients and complete directions on previous page

After making the dough in a food processor, shape into 4 balls and refrigerate for at least 1 hour.

Flatten 1 ball of dough with your palms on a well-floured surface. Then roll into an oval using a well-floured rolling pin, gently lifting and turning the dough once or twice, and adding more flour to the surface as needed, until you have a piece about 14 x 18 inches.

Add the filling to each piece of dough: first cinnamon, then sugar, walnuts, raisins, and preserves.

Use a pastry tool to fold over the edges on all four sides.

Gently loosen the dough from your surface as you roll lengthwise to the end of the dough.

Gently transfer filled dough to a parchment-lined cookie sheet. Scrape your surface clean before you roll and fill the next piece.

Spread room-temperature sour cream over the tops of the rolls before baking.

Let the baked strudel cool for an hour before cutting.

After trimming the ends (which are the chef's treat, of course), you'll get about 10 pieces of strudel from each roll.

Thumbprint Cookies

We still can't believe they're not butter cookies, and neither will you. The rich flavor of these little sweeties, filled with the preserve of your choice, produce a cookie that everyone seems to love.

Makes 4 dozen cookies

Ingredients

2 cups sifted all-purpose flour

½ teaspoon salt

2 Earth Balance Vegan Buttery Sticks

½ cup superfine sugar

1 teaspoon vanilla extract

1 teaspoon almond extract

jam or filling of your choice

½ cup sifted confectioners' sugar

Note
• Plan ahead, as the dough needs to chill for an hour or two.
• If you don't have superfine sugar, you can process granulated sugar in a dry blender or spice grinder until superfine.
• These cookies freeze well.

Method

1. In a small bowl, sift together flour and salt. Set aside.

2. In a mixer, cream the Earth Balance and sugar until mixture is light and fluffy.

3. Add both extracts and mix.

4. Slowly mix in the flour and salt mixture, half a cup at a time, until just blended. Don't overmix.

5. Wrap dough in plastic and chill for 1 to 2 hours.

6. Preheat oven to 325 degrees. Meanwhile, quickly shape the dough into 1-inch balls and space them 2 inches apart on an ungreased cookie sheet.

7. Make a deep thumbprint in the center of each, and fill with your preferred jam.

8. Bake for 10 to 15 minutes, or until cookies are the color of pale sand. Transfer to wire cooling racks.

9. When cooled, dust with confectioner's sugar.

Disappearing Oatmeal Cookies

The name pretty much speaks for itself. Soft and chewy and made with coconut, raisins, and cranberries, we try filling the cookie jar with these but they never hang around very long.

Makes 30 cookies

Ingredients

1½ Earth Balance Vegan Buttery Sticks

½ cup granulated sugar

1 cup packed light brown sugar

1 flax egg (1 flax egg = 1 tablespoon flaxseed soaked in 3 tablespoons warm water for 5 minutes)

2 tablespoons water

1 teaspoon vanilla extract

⅓ cup all-purpose flour

1 teaspoon ground cinnamon

½ teaspoon ground nutmeg

½ teaspoon salt

½ teaspoon baking soda

3 cups rolled oats

1 cup raisins

½ cup dried cranberries

½ cup unsweetened coconut flakes, toasted

Note
• Can make ahead. Store in an airtight container for 3 to 5 days.

Method

1. Preheat the oven to 350 degrees.

2. Line two cookie sheets with parchment paper.

3. Cream the Earth Balance and both sugars together until fluffy. Add the flax egg and mix to combine. Mix in the water and vanilla.

4. Sift together the flour, cinnamon, nutmeg, salt, and baking soda and mix into the wet ingredients. Add the oats, raisins, cranberries, and coconut and mix until well-combined, but don't overmix.

5. Using a 1-inch scoop, drop the dough onto the cookie sheets, leaving generous space around each cookie and pressing down lightly to flatten.

6. Bake for 8 to 10 minutes, until lightly brown. Do not overcook. Let rest on the pans for 5 minutes before transferring to a cooling rack.

Molasses Cookies

Depending on the kind of flour used, these cookies can be soft little drops (all-purpose flour) or crispy lace discs (gluten-free). Both are delicious.

Makes 3 dozen cookies

Ingredients

1½ Earth Balance Vegan Buttery Sticks, melted

1 cup sugar

¼ cup molasses

1 flax egg (1 flax egg = 1 tablespoon flaxseed soaked in 3 tablespoons warm water for 5 minutes)

1¾ cups gluten-free flour for lace cookies *or*
1¾ cups unbleached all-purpose flour for drop cookies

½ teaspoon ground cloves

1 teaspoon ground ginger

1 teaspoon ground cinnamon

½ teaspoon ground nutmeg

½ teaspoon salt

½ teaspoon baking soda

Method

1. Preheat the oven to 350 degrees.

2. In a large bowl, combine the melted Earth Balance, sugar, and molasses. Mix thoroughly.

3. Add the flax egg and mix.

4. In a bowl, sift together the flour, spices, salt, and baking soda. Add to the wet ingredients and mix.

5. Line a cookie sheet with foil, not parchment paper.

6. Using a teaspoon, drop the batter onto the foil, leaving space around each cookie.

7. Bake for 5 to 7 minutes. Remove from the oven when the cookies are still soft but beginning to darken.

8. Let cool on the cookie sheet for 10 minutes to firm up, then transfer to a cooling rack.

Chocolate Cookies with Peanut Butter "Nests"

Inspired by our friends at the Catskill Animal Sanctuary, these are easy to make and ideal for those aficionados of pairing chocolate with peanut butter. It's always nice to have another gluten-free cookie recipe on hand, but who would think it could taste so good.

Makes 2½ to 3 dozen cookies

For the chocolate dough

½ cup coconut oil, melted

1 cup sugar

¼ cup pure maple syrup

3 tablespoons unsweetened coconut milk

½ teaspoon vanilla extract

1½ cups chestnut flour

⅓ cup plus 2 tablespoons unsweetened cocoa powder

½ teaspoon baking soda

½ teaspoon salt

For the peanut butter filling

⅔ cup salted crunchy peanut butter

⅓ cup confectioners' sugar

1½ tablespoons unsweetened coconut milk

dash of vanilla extract

Note
• You can freeze leftover coconut milk; so if you are opening a new can for this recipe, don't worry about it going to waste.

Method

1. Preheat the oven to 350 degrees. Line a cookie sheet with parchment paper.

2. To make the chocolate dough, combine the coconut oil, sugar, maple syrup, coconut milk, and vanilla. Mix until smooth.

3. Sift together the chestnut flour, cocoa powder, baking soda, and salt and add to the bowl, mixing to form a moist dough. Do not overmix.

4. In another bowl, mix together all the peanut butter filling ingredients; the consistency should be like a moist, firm dough. If the filling becomes too dry, add more coconut milk, a little at a time. If the filling is too moist, knead in a little more confectioners' sugar.

5. Roll the peanut butter filling into tiny egg shapes.

6. Scoop approximately a tablespoon of chocolate dough into your hand, and using your thumb, indent the center to make a bowl shape. Place a peanut butter "egg" in the cookie "nest." Repeat using all the dough and "eggs."

7. Arrange the cookies on cookie sheet and chill in the fridge for 10 to 15 minutes.

8. Bake for 8 to 10 minutes until the chocolate cracks slightly.

9. Let cookies cool on the cookie sheet for about 5 minutes before transferring them to a wire rack to finish cooling.

Date Coconut Truffles

as trying to come up with a truffle recipe that didn't require using
recall how she came to this confection but assumes she must have had a
on hand because, she adds with a smile, "That's the way I cook." Add this
are looking for an easy yet special dessert that is suitable for any season.
ere's just enough decadence in each bite.

Makes 32 to 40 truffles

Ingredients

1 cup boiling water

2 cups chopped pitted dates

1 teaspoon vanilla extract

2 teaspoons pure maple syrup

pinch of salt

¾ cup coconut flour

3 tablespoons sifted cocoa powder

1⅔ cups chopped bittersweet chocolate

1½ cups unsweetened coconut flakes, toasted

Note
• In step 8, the truffles can also be rolled in chopped nuts or confectioner's sugar.
• Not only do these freeze well, they are delicious eaten right out of the freezer: The chocolate coating is crunchy and the center is creamy.

Method

1. Pour boiling water over the chopped dates and let stand 30 minutes, or until soft.

2. Put the dates and water in a food processor. Add the vanilla, maple syrup, and salt and purée until smooth, scraping down the sides of the processor.

3. Add the flour and cocoa and process, scraping down sides again, until you have a thick paste.

4. Transfer to a small bowl. Cover and refrigerate until very cold, about 3 hours.

5. Just before removing the mixture from the refrigerator, melt the chocolate in a double boiler on the stovetop.

6. Put the toasted coconut in a shallow bowl.

7. Remove the mixture from the refrigerator. Working in small batches, form the mix into truffle-sized balls using a 1-inch ice cream scoop.

8. Drop 1 ball at a time into the melted chocolate, turning with a fork to coat all sides. Pierce ball with the fork and shake off excess chocolate. Gently roll chocolate-covered ball in toasted coconut.

9. Place the truffle on a parchment-lined cookie sheet and repeat until all the balls are coated.

10. Refrigerate for at least 1 hour before serving.

Sauces and Dressings

Axis Mundi
on the northeast corner of the quarry pond.
Sculpture by Tom Gottsleben,
bluestone, stainless steel, and crystal

Basic Cashew Cream

For neutral or sweet dishes, you can make this dairy-free cream whatever consistency or sweetness is appropriate for the recipe. Add more water and you have a plant-based heavy cream. Sweeten it with honey or maple syrup, and add a flavoring such as vanilla, almond extract, or lemon zest. Once it's in your repertoire, you can vary it for many different uses.

Makes approximately 3½ cups

Ingredients

2 cups raw cashews, halves and pieces are fine

Water

Note
• Plan ahead: You need to put the cashews up to soak the night before you need the cashew cream.
• Refrigerates for 3 days; freezes for 1 month. You may need to reblend after freezing.
• For a thinner cream, add a bit more water to the food processor; for a thicker cream, add a little less.

Method

1. Rinse cashews under cold water, then cover with water and refrigerate overnight.

2. Drain cashews and rinse under cold water again.

3. Place cashews in a food processor and add enough water to cover them. Purée until you have desired consistency. Keep in mind that the cream will thicken in the refrigerator, but you can add a little more water as needed.

Diane's Sweet Potato Gingersnap Pie (page 198) gets its rich, creamy texture from Basic Cashew Cream.

Savory Cashew Cream Sauce

This is our go-to substitution in any recipe that calls for a butter- and flour-based sauce.

Makes approximately 2½ cups

Prepare in advance

Rinse cashews and soak in 2 cups warm water for an hour or more.

Ingredients

3 medium-size shallots, chopped

1 medium-size onion, chopped

3 cloves garlic, chopped

2 tablespoons coconut oil or grapeseed oil

4 carrots, chopped

3 stalks celery, chopped

1 cup raw cashews, soaked

3 tablespoons fresh lemon juice

pinch of cayenne pepper, or to taste

salt and freshly ground pepper

Method

1. On medium heat, sauté shallots, onion, and garlic in oil until soft.

2. Add carrots and celery and cook for a few minutes.

3. Add cashews and their soaking water and cook until vegetables are soft.

4. Remove from heat and let cool a few minutes, then blend in food processor until smooth.

5. Add lemon juice, cayenne pepper, salt, and pepper. Continue to blend in food processor until very smooth. Add more water to adjust the consistency of the sauce, if needed.

Note
• Can refrigerate for 3 days or freeze for 1 month.

Two dishes using Savory Cashew Cream Sauce:
Zucchini Feta Pancakes (below left, page 120) and Quintessential Mac and Cheese (below right, page 138).

Herb Vinaigrette

Makes approximately 1 cup

Ingredients

Any combination of chopped fresh herbs: basil, parsley, chives, dill, etc.

2 cloves garlic, chopped

1 teaspoon Dijon mustard

1 tablespoon honey, or to taste (optional)

salt and freshly ground pepper

⅓ cup balsamic vinegar

⅔ cup olive oil

Method

1. In a food processor or blender, layer herbs, garlic, mustard, and honey. Season with salt and pepper, add the vinegar and blend.

2. Slowly add the olive oil. Adjust seasoning to taste.

Note
• If your balsamic vinegar is on the sweet side, you might choose to omit the honey.

Lemon Vinaigrette

Whisk all ingredients together.

Makes approximately 1 cup

Ingredients

2 cloves garlic, minced

zest of 1 lemon

2 tablespoons fresh lemon juice

1 teaspoon Dijon mustard

1 teaspoon honey

2 tablespoons wine vinegar

6 tablespoons olive oil

1 tablespoon chopped fresh dill or basil

1 tablespoon chopped flat-leaf parsley

Asian Vinaigrette

Whisk all the ingredients together.

Makes approximately ½ cup

Ingredients

3 scallions, chopped

3 cloves garlic, chopped

2 tablespoons finely grated fresh ginger

2 tablespoons brown rice vinegar

3 tablespoons plum vinegar

2 tablespoons mirin

3 tablespoons shoyu soy sauce

2½ tablespoons grapeseed oil

3 dashes toasted sesame oil

1 tablespoon chopped fresh cilantro

Creamy Citrus-Chive Dipping Sauce

Simply mix all the ingredients together.

Makes approximately 2 cups

Ingredients

12 ounces vegan sour cream

half of a 6-ounce container vegan cream cheese

juice of 2 limes

juice of 1 lemon

3 tablespoons finely chopped chives, or more to taste

½ teaspoon Sriracha-style hot sauce

salt and freshly ground pepper to taste

Carrot Tahini Dressing

Makes approximately 2 cups

Ingredients

enough carrots, juiced, to make 1½ cups liquid *or* 1½ cups carrot juice

6 large cloves garlic

½ cup grated fresh ginger

2 tablespoons chopped fresh Thai basil

2 tablespoons chopped flat-leaf parsley

½ tablespoon chopped fresh chives

salt and freshly ground pepper

2 tablespoons tahini

½ cup Bragg Liquid Aminos

¼ cup rice wine vinegar

2 tablespoons fresh lemon juice

3 tablespoons sesame oil

2 avocados (optional, see note)

Method

Blend all the ingredients in a food processor or blender.

Note
• Avocados make this dressing creamy. If using them, add just before serving.

Chimichurri

This versatile green sauce comes from Argentina. The thick, smooth version made in the blender, as described here, is great to drizzle over cooked foods (eggplant, tofu, portobello mushrooms) just before serving, or as a condiment on the table. Thinned with a little water or olive oil, you can use it as a marinade or for basting foods while grilling.

Makes approximately 1 cup

Ingredients

1 bunch flat-leaf parsley *or* ½ bunch cilantro and ½ bunch parsley

8 cloves garlic, minced

1 tablespoon diced red onion

1 teaspoon dried oregano

1 teaspoon freshly ground pepper

½ teaspoon salt

¼ cup red wine vinegar

1 tablespoon fresh lemon juice

¾ cup extra-virgin olive oil

Method

1. Chop parsley (and cilantro if using) in a food processor.

2. Add the remaining ingredients and blend until smooth.

Note
• Refrigerates for up to 5 days.
• Freezes well.

Ginger-Tamari Dipping Sauce

Mix all the ingredients together. Let sit for at least a half hour to allow the flavors to meld.

Makes approximately 1 cup

Ingredients

½ cup tamari

½ cup water

2 teaspoons minced fresh ginger

2 large cloves garlic, minced

1½ tablespoons pure maple syrup

1 teaspoon mirin

Roasted Pepper and Tomato Confit

Makes approximately 1 cup

Ingredients

1 head of garlic

2 large tomatoes

2 red bell peppers

¼ cup olive oil

salt and freshly ground pepper to taste

¾ cup red wine vinegar

1 whole sprig of oregano

1 whole sprig of thyme

1 tablespoon honey

Note
• Refrigerates for 3 to 5 days.

Method

1. Preheat the oven to 375 degrees. Roast the garlic, as described on page 242.

2. While roasting the garlic, also roast the tomatoes and peppers separately, each tossed with oil, salt, and pepper for 20 to 25 minutes, or until charred.

3. When the tomatoes and peppers are cool enough to handle, peel, seed, and chop them separately. Set aside.

4. In a small saucepan, combine the vinegar with the roasted tomatoes, roasted garlic pulp, and herbs. Cook until the tomatoes break down, about 20 minutes. Add the roasted peppers and simmer for another 15 minutes. Remove the herb sprigs. Season with salt and pepper to taste.

5. Purée using an immersion blender or food processor, then stir in honey.

Aioli

Makes approximately 1 cup

Ingredients

½ cup slivered almonds

1 head of garlic, roasted, page 242

¾ cup Roasted Red Peppers, page 242, or Oven-Dried Tomatoes, page 243 (or substitute store-bought)

1 tablespoon Dijon mustard

3 tablespoons lemon juice

3 tablespoons water

salt and freshly ground pepper

Method

1. Toast the almonds on the stovetop.

2. Squeeze the garlic from the roasted bulb.

3. Put all the ingredients except water in a food processor and process 1 minute or until smooth.

4. Gradually add the water until you have a smooth mayonnaise-like consistency.

5. Season with salt and pepper to taste.

Patty's Special Sauce

Mix together all the ingredients. If the sauce is too thick, add ¼ cup water.

Makes approximately 4 ½ cups

4 cups Organic Vegenaise

3 tablespoons Dijon mustard

2 tablespoons nutritional yeast

3 tablespoons fresh lemon juice

1½ tablespoons olive oil

3 tablespoons Worcestershire sauce

4 to 5 cloves garlic, pressed in garlic press

freshly ground pepper

Russian Dressing

Mix together all the ingredients.

Makes approximately 1 quart

Ingredients

1 teaspoon ground black pepper

2 cups Just Mayo

1 cup ketchup

2 tablespoons Dijon mustard

1 tablespoon Worcestershire sauce

2 tablespoons fresh lemon juice

1 tablespoon capers, drained

2 tablespoons prepared horseradish

½ cup chopped pickles (sweet, kosher, or dill)

¼ cup finely chopped red onion

Tzatziki Sauce

Mix together all the ingredients and refrigerate for a half hour so the flavors will meld.

Makes approximately 1½ cups

Ingredients

2 cups vegan sour cream

2 cloves garlic, minced

juice of ½ lemon

2 cucumbers, seeded, peeled, and finely chopped or grated

mint, dill, or cilantro, finely chopped (optional)

3 tablespoons chopped scallions

salt and freshly ground pepper to taste

Rafferty's Puttanesca Sauce

Makes approximately 4 cups

Ingredients

½ large onion, finely chopped

3 tablespoons olive oil

5 cloves garlic, finely chopped

½ pound sliced mushrooms

1 eggplant, peeled and cubed

2 tablespoons capers, plus a teaspoon of their juice

½ teaspoon red pepper flakes

2 (28-ounce) cans of whole San Marzano tomatoes

½ cup chopped flat-leaf parsley

¼ cup chopped fresh basil leaves (or 1 teaspoon dried)

½ to 1 teaspoon sugar, if needed

½ cup olives (we mix Kalamata and oil-cured), pitted and cut in half, and a little juice from the container

salt and freshly ground pepper to taste

Note
• Can make ahead: Refrigerates well for up to 5 days.
• Freezes well.

Method

1. In a large pot, sauté the onion in the olive oil until golden brown.

2. Add the garlic and mushrooms and stir to combine. Add the eggplant. Cook until browned.

3. Add the capers, red pepper flakes, and tomatoes with their juice. Bring to a slow boil.

4. Stir in the herbs, sugar, if using, and olives.

5. Lower the heat and simmer for 1 hour, stirring occasionally. Add salt and pepper and adjust other seasonings to taste.

A whimsical, mellow Airedale, Rafferty was with Patty and Tom for seven years before his sudden death in 1988. It was the process of making a memorial bench for Rafferty that inspired Tom, then a painter, to see with new eyes the bluestone that was everywhere on their property. The following year he began making stone sculpture and he and Patty launched a sculpture business called Rafferty Rocks. In time, the Spiral House was created as a stone sculpture large enough to live in and Tom's Rainbow sculpture came to define the hillside above Rafferty's Bench. Now, the cookbook you are holding is the first title from Rafferty Rocks Press. As so often happens, loss and grief became the door to new possibilities.

Roasted Garden Marinara Sauce

We should admit at the outset that Diane takes two days to make this sauce. But the result is a little bit of heaven over pasta. Made fresh from the late summer harvest, or taken from the freezer for a winter meal, this dish epitomizes delicious abundance.

Makes approximately 8 cups

Ingredients

8 to 10 cups wedges of fresh garden tomatoes (cores removed)

1 cup olive oil

15 cloves garlic, peeled

6 to 8 fresh basil leaves

leaves of 1 small bunch flat-leaf parsley

salt and freshly ground pepper to taste

1 large onion, thinly sliced

½ pound mushrooms, stemmed and sliced

2 carrots, peeled and shredded

1 large zucchini, cut in chunks

1 eggplant, peeled and cut in chunks

Note
• Refrigerates well.
• Freezes well.

Method

1. Preheat the oven to 375 degrees.

2. Place the tomatoes in a large heavy pot. Add ¾ cup of the olive oil, garlic, basil, parsley, salt, and pepper. Stir. Roast uncovered for 30 minutes.

3. Reduce temperature to 325 degrees and roast for another 3½ hours. At this point, the tomatoes should begin to look oily.

4. While the tomatoes are roasting, sauté the onion, mushroom, carrot, zucchini, and eggplant in the remaining ¼ cup olive oil until the onions are translucent and the veggies are soft. Set aside.

5. After the tomatoes have finished roasting, use an immersion blender to process them, chunky or smooth depending on your taste. (You can also use a food processor or countertop blender.)

6. Add the sautéed veggies from step 4 to the tomatoes. Return to the oven for another 1½ hours.

Marinara Sauce

When tomatoes are out of season, good canned tomatoes make a great marinara. We like the ones named for the San Marzano region in southern Italy where they grow.

Makes approximately 4 cups

Ingredients

½ large onion, finely chopped

3 cloves garlic, finely chopped

¼ cup olive oil

2 (28-ounce) cans of whole San Marzano tomatoes

½ teaspoon sugar

4 fresh basil leaves *or* 1 teaspoon dried basil

¼ cup chopped flat-leaf parsley

salt and freshly ground pepper to taste

Method

1. In a large pot, sauté the chopped onion and garlic in olive oil on low heat until golden brown.

2. Add the tomatoes and their juice and bring to a slow boil. Use a potato masher to break up the tomatoes as they cook.

3. Add the sugar, basil, and parsley. Stir.

4. Simmer for 1½ hours, stirring occasionally. Season with salt and pepper to taste.

Note
• Can make ahead: Refrigerates well for up to 5 days.
• Freezes well.

Polenta Greens Casserole
(page 146) with Marinara Sauce.

Basil Pesto

Makes approximately 1 cup

Ingredients

1 cup pine nuts (or walnuts or cashews)

1½ cups chopped fresh basil

⅓ cup olive oil

6 large cloves garlic

⅓ cup nutritional yeast

1 teaspoon salt

½ teaspoon freshly ground pepper

Method

1. Toast the nuts in a skillet on the stovetop.

2. Combine all the ingredients and pulse in a food processor until the nuts are ground. The pesto should still have texture.

3. Add more salt and pepper to taste, if needed.

Note
• There are so many ways to vary this pesto: Stir in chopped, Oven-Dried Tomatoes (page 243) after everything else is processed. Use Roasted Garlic (page 242) instead of raw. Combine chopped flat-leaf parsley with the basil.

The exuberant energy of garlic scapes (facing page) inspired Tom to create this sculpture. And even though the bluestone Scapes are fixed in space, they seem to dance as unpredictably as their garden namesakes.

Kale and Garlic Scapes Pesto

Hardneck garlic plants send out shoots that twist and wind into whimsically loopy shapes. Garlic growers pick the scapes while the seed pod is small and tight, so the plant will send its energy into fattening the underground bulb rather than ripening the flower and setting seed. These cut stalks have an intense garlic flavor that makes a delicious pesto, especially when combined with the tender young garden kale that is in season at the same time — in June in our Northeast climate. The scapes will keep in the refrigerator for several weeks.

Makes approximately 2 cups

Prepare in advance

Nutty Parm, page 241

Ingredients

4 cups coarsely chopped kale

3 cups coarsely chopped garlic scapes

3 cups fresh basil leaves

1 cup flat-leaf parsley

3 tablespoons fresh lemon juice

2 cups Nutty Parm

1 to 1½ cups olive oil

salt and freshly ground pepper to taste

Method

In a food processor, blend the kale, garlic scapes, herbs, lemon juice, and Nutty Parm, adding the olive oil slowly to make a nice, creamy paste. Season with salt and pepper to taste.

Mushroom Gravy

The key to a good mushroom gravy is to leave the mushrooms alone while they brown — don't even add any salt and pepper — and stir only enough to keep them from burning. This way the mushrooms hold their flavor. Of course you also want to start with good fresh mushrooms.

Makes 2 to 2½ cups

Ingredients

½ pound shiitake mushrooms, sliced

½ pound oyster mushrooms, sliced

3 tablespoons Earth Balance Vegan Buttery Stick

1 small onion, diced

3 large cloves garlic, chopped

½ teaspoon fresh thyme

1 tablespoon nutritional yeast

salt and freshly ground pepper

3 to 4 tablespoons all-purpose flour

½ cup white wine

1 cup vegetable stock (If the menu includes anything with boiled potato, use the potato water as the stock.)

Method

1. Sauté both types of mushrooms in the Earth Balance over low-medium heat until lightly brown.

2. Add the onion, garlic, thyme, nutritional yeast, salt, and pepper and continue to cook, stirring occasionally, until the vegetables are soft.

3. Add 3 tablespoons of the flour and stir several times while the flour cooks, approximately 5 minutes, to make a light roux. Add the fourth tablespoon of flour if needed.

4. Add the white wine and slowly add the stock, stirring as you add the stock to prevent lumps from forming.

5. Cook on low heat for 8 to 10 minutes, stirring occasionally.

6. Remove from heat, and serve with any kind of potato mash, polenta, roasted tempeh, or tofu.

Thanksgiving Cranberry Chutney

Makes approximately 2 cups

Ingredients

2 (8-ounce) bags organic cranberries

1 onion, minced

2 tablespoons Earth Balance Vegan Buttery Stick

1 apple, cored and chopped

¼ cup pomegranate juice (or orange or cranberry juice)

½ cup maple syrup

2 tablespoons grated fresh ginger

1 teaspoon ground cumin

juice of 1 lemon

juice of 2 oranges

¼ cup dark rum

¼ cup toasted pine nuts or chopped toasted walnuts

Note
• Can make ahead: Refrigerates well for up to 3 days.
• Freezes well.

Method

1. In a large pan, cook the cranberries and onions in Earth Balance until the cranberries pop.

2. Add the remaining ingredients and simmer until well combined, approximately 15 minutes.

Proud
to be an
American

Born in Trapani, Italy, 56 years ago, Joe Santamaria, Tom's logistics coordinator, became an American citizen at the State Supreme Court in Kingston, New York, on September 4, 2015. What a perfect excuse for a party. We celebrated with carrot dogs on buns with all the trimmings, potato salad, grilled vegetables fresh from the garden, and sweet corn on the cob from our own Hudson Valley, known for some of the best in the country. And lots of friends and animals, of course.

Etc

Chrysalis
Sculpture by Tom Gottsleben,
bluestone, stainless steel, and crystal.

Italian Rub

We use this rub when grilling or roasting vegetables that are either tender or mild in flavor, such as radicchio, endive, fennel, and zucchini.

Makes approximately ¼ cup

Ingredients

2 tablespoons "Italian seasonings" (mix of basil, oregano, rosemary, and thyme)

2 teaspoons salt

1 teaspoon freshly ground pepper

1 tablespoon granulated garlic

½ teaspoon onion powder

Note
• Both rubs can be stored in the freezer in an air-tight container.

Roasting Rub

This is the rub we use when grilling or roasting heartier foods such as portobello mushrooms, eggplant, tempeh, and tofu.

Makes approximately ⅔ cup

Ingredients

¼ cup organic turbinado sugar (You can use brown sugar, but it will burn; turbinado won't.)

2 tablespoons paprika

2 tablespoons freshly ground pepper

2 tablespoons salt

1 tablespoon granulated garlic

1 tablespoon onion powder

1 teaspoon celery seed

½ teaspoon cayenne pepper

1 teaspoon ground cumin

2 tablespoons ground turmeric

Nutty Parm

This is our vegan "parmesan cheese."

Makes approximately 1 cup

Ingredients

1 cup brazil nuts

1 cup cashew nuts

¼ cup nutritional yeast

salt and pepper to taste

Method

1. Toast nuts in a 350-degree oven for 10 minutes. Let cool slightly.

2. Combine all ingredients in a food processor and pulse until you have the consistency of grated cheese.

Note
• Can refrigerate for 2 weeks.
• Freezes well.

Maple-Glazed Walnuts

Ingredients

2 cups walnuts

2 tablespoons Earth Balance Vegan Buttery Stick

2 tablespoons olive oil

salt and freshly ground pepper

6 tablespoons maple syrup

cooking spray (grapeseed, canola, or other neutral oil)

Method

1. Toast the walnuts in a dry frying pan for a few minutes to bring out the oils. Be careful not to burn.

2. Heat the Earth Balance and olive oil in a skillet over medium heat. Add the toasted walnuts and cook for approximately 2 minutes, stirring frequently. Add salt, pepper, and maple syrup and stir until the nuts are well-coated and begin to caramelize, approximately 4 minutes more.

3. Line a baking sheet with parchment paper and spray with cooking oil. Transfer the walnuts to the baking sheet, separating the nuts so they don't stick together. Let cool.

Roasted Garlic

Method

1. Preheat the oven to 350 degrees.

2. Cut off the top of a garlic bulb.

3. Place the bulb on foil, cut side facing up, and sprinkle with salt, freshly ground pepper, and olive oil. Wrap tightly in foil.

4. Roast for 45 minutes. Cool slightly.

5. Squeeze the garlic from the bulb to use in a recipe, or serve on the table with a cocktail-size fork.

Roasted Red Peppers

Method

1. Coat whole red peppers with olive oil and cook directly over a gas flame on a stovetop, on an outside grill, or on a baking sheet in a preheated 400-degree oven. Char the outsides of the peppers on all sides until blackened.

2. Place in a paper bag to steam for approximately 15 minutes, which helps the skin come away from the peppers.

3. Remove peppers from the bag and peel off the skin.

4. Cut open the peppers and remove and discard the seeds and ribs. Slice or chop to the desired size.

Note
- Serve roasted garlic warm or cool.
- Keeps in refrigerator up to 3 days.

Oven-Dried Tomatoes

Ingredients

3 pounds cherry tomatoes, each cut in half lengthwise

olive oil, to lightly sprinkle over tomatoes

salt and freshly ground pepper

2 tablespoon sugar (if tomatoes are not in season)

Note
• Try to use tomatoes of similar size, or some will overcook before others are ready.
• Freezes well.

Method

1. Preheat the oven to 200 degrees.

2. Line a baking sheet with parchment paper.

3. Slice tomatoes in half. Place on baking sheet cut side up.

4. Drizzle with olive oil and sprinkle with salt and pepper, and sugar if needed.

5. Roast for 1½ hours or longer, checking frequently. You want tomatoes to dry and brown but not burn. Cook until juices stop running, edges are shriveled, and pieces have shrunken slightly.

6. Cool tomatoes and freeze overnight on the baking sheet. Transfer tomatoes into freezer bags and return to freezer until ready to use.

Pickled Onions

Makes 6 cups

Ingredients

3 medium-size red onions, thinly sliced

½ cup grapeseed oil

juice of 3 small limes

1 tablespoon chopped fresh dill

3 small jalapeño peppers, seeded and chopped (can substitute 3 pickled jalapeños, seeded and chopped)

1 teaspoon salt

3 teaspoons freshly ground pepper

⅓ cup umeboshi plum vinegar

⅓ cup sherry vinegar

3 tablespoons raw sugar

Method

1. In a large bowl, combine the onions, oil, lime juice, dill, jalapeños, salt, and pepper.

2. In a small saucepan, heat both vinegars with the sugar, stirring occasionally, until the sugar dissolves. Pour over the onion mixture and stir to combine.

3. Cover and let stand at room temperature for 12 to 24 hours, depending on how strong you want the flavors. Refrigerate until ready to use.

Note
• Can refrigerate for up to 2 weeks.

Onion Relish

Serves 6

Ingredients

4 large onions, Vidalia or red, thinly sliced

2 tablespoons grapeseed oil

2 large cloves garlic, finely chopped

1 teaspoon salt

2 tablespoons chopped fresh rosemary

¼ cup balsamic vinegar

1 tablespoon umeboshi plum vinegar

3 tablespoons honey

Method

1. In a large saucepan, sauté the onions in the oil over medium heat until they brown and caramelize, approximately 15 minutes.

2. Lower the heat and add the garlic, salt, and rosemary. Cook for 15 to 20 minutes more, stirring occasionally and taking care not to burn the garlic.

3. Stir in both vinegars and the honey.

4. Remove from heat and allow to cool.

Note
• Stored in a glass jar in the refrigerator, this will keep for up to 2 weeks.

Vegetable Stock

...aries with the ingredients you have on hand and the flavor you want for ...d, this version is one that Diane makes in large quantities and freezes as ...later. The potatoes give it body, the string beans add a great flavor, the ...r earthiness. The fennel trimmings are a relatively new addition, the result of na... ...fennel around and discovering how much flavor it added to the stockpot.

Makes 2 quarts

Ingredients

2 onions, halved

1 leek, roots removed, sliced vertically down the center, washed well

2 cloves garlic, peeled and left whole

2 cups string beans, stem side removed, left whole

4 dried shiitake mushrooms, left whole, or stems from any mushrooms left over from another recipe

4 stalks celery, cut in big chunks

2 carrots, cut in big chunks

3 to 4 white potatoes, peeled and cut in chunks

1 bunch flat-leaf parsley

1 bay leaf

2 sprigs thyme

trimmings from 2 to 3 fennel bulbs

½ cup white wine or water *or* 3 tablespoons Bragg Liquid Amino, for deglazing roasting pan

6 quarts water

salt and freshly ground pepper to taste

Method

1. Preheat the oven to 375 degrees.

2. Oven-roast all the ingredients except the deglazing liquid and water for approximately 1 hour.

3. When the vegetables are almost caramelized, transfer them to a stockpot.

4. Add the wine, water, or Bragg to the roasting pan and stir, scraping up the bits of vegetables from the bottom of the pan. If using wine, let the liquid cook down a little bit.

5. Add the 6 quarts water to the roasted vegetables. Cover the stockpot and bring to a boil, then reduce the heat and simmer, covered, for 45 minutes to an hour. Add salt and pepper to taste.

6. Strain the stock and use immediately or freeze once cooled.

Note
• Add vegetables that support or complement the flavors of the dish you are making — asparagus trimmings for asparagus soup, corn cobs for corn chowder, the skins and seeds of winter squash for soups featuring those vegetables.
• Avoid vegetables in the cabbage family, which tend to make stock bitter and gassy over the long cooking time required.
• Don't use old vegetables. If you wouldn't eat it as a vegetable, don't put it in the stockpot.
• Don't over-caramelize the vegetables.
• Freezes well for approximately 6 months.

Diane's Piecrust

Makes two 9-inch piecrusts

Ingredients

2½ cups all-purpose flour

1 tablespoon sugar (omit if making crust for a savory pie)

1 teaspoon salt

¾ cup (1½ sticks) cold Earth Balance Vegan Buttery Sticks, cut into ¼-inch cubes

½ cup (1 stick) cold Earth Balance Vegan Shortening, cut into 4 pieces

¼ cup cold water

3 tablespoons cold vodka (ensures a flakier crust)

Note
• To prebake a piecrust before filling, see "Blind Baking" on the facing page.

Method

1. In a large mixing bowl, whisk together the flour, sugar, and salt. Cut in the Earth Balance butter and shortening just until you have small crumbles. Mixing longer will produce a mealy, tough crust.

2. Stir in the chilled water and vodka a little at a time, gently tossing with your fingers.

3. When the dough is mixed, quickly gather it into a rough ball and divide it in half. Wrap each half in plastic wrap and refrigerate for at least 30 minutes.

4. Unwrap one-half of the chilled dough and place it on a 12- x 12-inch sheet of parchment paper. Cover the dough with another sheet of parchment paper of the same size.

5. Starting in the middle of the flattened dough, press down gently on your rolling pin and roll away from yourself with even strokes, turning the parchment paper occasionally, until the dough round reaches the edges of the paper.

6. Remove the top layer of the paper and flip the dough over carefully into the pie plate. Remove the other piece of parchment paper and press the dough into the pie plate.

7. Cut off excess dough so that ½ inch extends beyond the pie plate. Use the tines of a fork to decorate the edges or pinch with your fingers as shown in photo at left.

8. Fill your piecrust (see note).

9. For a two-crust pie, roll out the second crust, cover the filling, and cut several slits in the top. Or cut the second crust in strips to make a lattice topping for the pie.

10. Bake according to the needs of the filling, being careful not to overcook the crust.

Blind Baking

For pies with custard fillings, prebaking the crust keeps it from getting soggy.

Ingredients

1 piecrust shell in a pie plate

Method

1. Cover the pie shell with aluminum foil and weight it down with dried beans or a pie weight. (Beans are not edible after this use.)

2. Bake in a preheated 425-degree oven for 20 minutes.

3. Remove the foil and beans and bake for 5 minutes more or until lightly browned.

Nut and Date Crust

This is a great gluten-free option for any fruit or pudding-style pie.

Makes one 9-inch crust

Ingredients

1 cup raw pecans

½ cup raw cashews

½ cup pumpkin seeds

½ cup dried dates, stems removed (You can substitute figs for dates.)

½ cup dried cranberries

1 teaspoon vanilla extract

dash of salt

½ teaspoon ground cinnamon

Method

1. Toast the nuts in the oven or on the stovetop. If the different nuts (or pieces of nuts) are all the same size, you can toast them together. Toast the pumpkin seeds separately.

2. Pulse all the ingredients together in a food processor until you are able to pinch the mixture together. If it's not moist enough, add a few drops of water.

3. Press the nut mixture evenly into the bottom and sides of a 9-inch pie plate.

4. The crust is ready to fill now or can be refrigerated and filled later.

Note
• Can be eaten raw or baked (time and temperature would depend on the filling).
• If baking, grease the pie plate before adding crust.

Tom's Smoothies

For more than five years now, Tom has looked forward to his daily green smoothie, which has pretty much remained unchanged all this time. It's hard to improve on perfection, so we blend up several days' worth at a time in our Vitamix. With its base of cucumbers, celery, apples, and grapes, it's both refreshing and light, ideal for breakfast or an afternoon snack, and Patty and Andrea have been known to add some rum to theirs at the end of the day.

Makes 4 smoothies, 10 ounces each

Ingredients

12 ounces apple cider

½ to 1 large cucumber, peeled and chopped in pieces

1 apple, cored, sliced, and chopped

1 kiwi, peeled and chopped

1 stalk broccoli, chopped

6 leaves kale, stems removed

2 stalks celery, chopped

juice of 1 lemon

1½ cups frozen grapes

Method

Combine all the ingredients in a powerful blender and process until smooth.

Coffee Break Granola

Makes approximately 10 cups

Ingredients

1½ cups apple cider

¾ cup pure maple syrup

2 teaspoons vanilla extract

2 tablespoons grapeseed or coconut oil

1 cup almonds, chopped

1 cup walnuts, chopped

1 cup cashews, chopped

¼ cup flaxseed, ground

¾ cup pumpkin seeds

1 cup shredded unsweetened coconut

6 cups rolled oats

2 tablespoons ground cinnamon

1 tablespoon ground nutmeg

1 teaspoon salt

1 cup dried fruit of your choice
(raisins, cranberries, cherries, etc.)

Method

1. Preheat the oven to 350 degrees.

2. In a saucepan, heat and reduce apple cider by half.

3. Stir in the maple syrup, vanilla, and oil. Remove from the heat.

4. Toast the nuts and seeds separately on a baking sheet in the oven until lightly brown.

5. Toast the shredded coconut on a cookie sheet until lightly brown.

6. In a large bowl, combine oats with the cinnamon, nutmeg, salt, and the nuts (but not the seeds). Pour in the reduced liquid and toss to combine.

7. Put the mixture on a parchment-lined baking sheet and bake for 15 to 30 minutes, until slightly brown. Watch carefully and use a spatula to fold the edges toward the center and the center out toward the edges so everything bakes evenly without burning.

8. Remove from the oven and toss in the dried fruit, toasted coconut, and seeds. Let cool completely before storing.

Note
• Can store in an airtight container for up to 2 weeks.

What is it about cooking that makes us want to share what we learn and love? Maybe it's because food is such a universal language, or because the way we cook and the food we favor is part of what makes each of us unique. Or perhaps it's because the time we spend eating and cooking with family and friends is one of our most frequent experiences of community. And what is community if not sharing? The following are a mix of favorite tips from Chef Diane and the Spiral House cookbook crew (Patty, Val, Jane, Sara, Ronnie, and Andrea). We hope these ideas will help you get the most out of your plant-based kitchen. And remember that cooking is very much like anything else: The more you do it, the better you become. And the more you'll have to share. *Bon appétit.*

Protein Charts

If you are transitioning to a plant-based diet (or already follow a vegan diet and want to ensure that your daily protein intake is adequate), print out a comprehensive protein chart — you'll find one at *www.vrg.org/nutrition/protein.php*. At first, pay attention to the meals you plan and what you are eating in the course of a day. Notice how you feel, too. Soon, you will have demystified plant-based protein and getting enough will be instinctive.

Getting enough protein

If you switch to a plant-based diet, or even dare to reduce the amount of animal protein that you eat, prepare to be bombarded with questions from well-meaning relatives and friends about how, exactly, you plan to get enough protein.

Americans are obsessed with protein with many convinced that a high-protein/low-carb diet is the panacea for weight loss. We actually need much less protein than we think, however, and much less than most Americans eat. The scientific community is now largely in agreement that vegans can easily meet their protein needs if their diets are varied and their calorie intake is adequate.

Only about one calorie out of every ten we eat needs to come from protein and the amounts we need change as we age. The approximate daily requirements are: babies, about 10 grams, school-age kids 19 to 34 grams, teenage boys up to 52 grams, teenage girls about 46 grams, adult men about 56 grams, adult women about 46 grams, and pregnant or breastfeeding women about 71 grams.

Good sources of plant-based protein include tempeh, lentils, beans (including chickpeas, cooked soybeans, and edamame), tofu, quinoa, peas, peanut and other nut butters, almonds, sunflower seeds, whole wheat bread, oatmeal, soy milk, spinach, broccoli, and kale. Nuts are a good source of protein, and their fats are mostly the heart-healthy monounsaturated kind; but because they are high in calories they should be eaten in moderation.

Some people have difficulty digesting **beans**. This doesn't mean you should avoid beans; they are a terrific protein source. The following varieties are considered easier to digest: black-eyed peas, adzuki, red lentils, mung, and perhaps, chickpeas and black beans. It's a myth that soaking or precooking beans will reduce digestive issues, but it will reduce the cooking time.

Seitan, a highly-concentrated source of protein, is made from wheat gluten, thus it is not suitable for those on wheat- or gluten-free diets. Also known as "wheat meat," seitan is prepared by soaking or boiling wheat flour to remove its sugars and starches, and then filtering it multiple times to produce a dense, somewhat rubbery product that is generally precooked before reaching the consumer. We limit its use at the Spiral House because some people here are on gluten-free diets. We also pay careful attention to our choice of wheats because we question the composition of today's hybridized wheat, which bears little resemblance to what our grandparents and even our parents ate. Einkorn, the most primitive species of wheat available today, is thought to be more easily digested by some people with digestive problems.

Preparing tempeh

Tempeh is a versatile and nutrient-rich protein staple in any plant-based kitchen. Like tofu, it is made from soybeans, but the two are prepared very differently. Tofu is made by curdling fresh, hot soy milk with a coagulant and tempeh is produced by fermenting cooked soybeans with a mold. Tempeh also has an entirely different texture (firm, dense,

There are different schools of thought when it comes to **soaking beans** before cooking. Diane prefers to "quick-soak" them by bringing them to a boil and simmering for one to three minutes, after which she turns off the burner and allows them to rest in the hot water, covered, for an hour before cooking. When cooking, she does not salt the water until the end.

Everyone at the Spiral House loves the way Diane makes **tempeh**, including the omnivores among us. Sometimes it is served as shown here, as a side of protein, and sometimes as part of a more complex recipe. (See the preparation description at right.)

We limit the amount of **tofu** (and other non-fermented soy) in our diets. But we do enjoy it as part of a mixed grill. Those are garlic scapes serving as tasty skewers in the photo.

and chewy), flavor (yeasty, nutty) and nutritional composition (protein, dietary fiber, and vitamins). A B_{12} bonanza, it has the benefits of all healthy fermented foods that are friendly to our guts. (See more about the advantages of fermentation further on in this section.)

Tempeh comes in cakes that freeze well and defrost quickly, which makes it convenient to keep a supply on hand. Diane places packaged frozen tempeh in a bowl of room-temperature water for a few minutes to begin defrosting it. With a sharp knife, she can slice or cube it even before it is fully defrosted. She then simmers the tempeh before the final preparation. This softens the inherently tough texture and also allows the tempeh to absorb the flavorings of the marinade or seasonings. Her technique:

• In a sauté pan, boil enough water to cover the tempeh. Diane might add some ginger or garlic to the water, depending on how she plans to use the tempeh.

• Add the tempeh, reduce heat to a simmer, and cook uncovered for 15 minutes.

• Drain tempeh and season for your recipe. If Diane is including it in an Asian meal, she might marinate it with toasted sesame oil and soy sauce. If it's part of an Italian meal, then she'll season it with basil, oregano, and parsley.

Using this approach, you can prepare tempeh as the protein for any meal. See our Puréed Cauliflower with Swiss Chard and Tempeh (page 132) and Tempeh Madeira (page 134).

Preparing tofu
Diane has a simple system for removing the excess water from tofu.

• Spread paper towels or linen dish towels on a baking sheet, place the sliced tofu on the towels in a single layer, cover with more paper or linen towels, and place a second baking sheet on the top.

• Using books or cans of food, evenly weight the top baking sheet for about one-half to one hour for use in a quick stir-fry, two to two-and-a-half hours if you are planning to marinate and bake the tofu.

• Another tip: Freezing and defrosting tofu before pressing out the moisture adds a chewy texture that enhances some dishes, such as Tom's Cottage Pie (page 158).

Organic vs. conventional

Once available only in health food stores, organic food is now widely sold in supermarkets, farmers' markets, and even through urban food delivery services. The term "organic" refers to food that is cultivated or processed without the use of chemicals — including fertilizers, insecticides, and herbicides — or artificial colorings, flavorings, or additives. Organic farming practices are also designed to reduce pollution and encourage soil and water conservation.

The United States Department of Agriculture (USDA) has created certification requirements so that, legally, any product labeled "organic" must be USDA certified. Products that are completely organic may be labeled "100 percent organic" in addition to bearing the "organic" seal. Foods certified as 95 percent or more organic may carry the "USDA Organic" seal. Products that contain at least 70 percent organic ingredients can only say "made with organic ingredients" on their labels. Products with less than 70 percent organic ingredients may not use the organic seal but may identify specific organic ingredients.

Producers whose gross agricultural income from organic sales is $5,000 or less — like some at your local farmers' market — are exempt from certification. The terms "natural," "free-range," "hormone-free," and "non-GMO" do not mean that a product or food is organic.

Consumer Reports offers a helpful explanation of price lookup codes (PLU numbers) on those little labels on your produce (*consumerreports.org/cro/news/2010/05/what-do-plu-codes-say-about-your-produce/index.htm*). The piece decodes the

We are blessed to have bountiful **organic vegetable gardens**. And we are also blessed to live in a community where health food stores, farmstands, and seasonal farmers' markets offer local, sustainably grown, and largely organic produce. These businesses are crucial for the health of the larger community, and as increasing numbers of people see the importance of eating this way and supporting local commerce, the prices will be more in line with conventionally-produced food. It is already happening.

...etables that are most free
...sidue, with the cleanest at
... list:

Avocado
Corn
Pineapple
Cabbage
Sweet peas (frozen)
Onions
Asparagus
Mangos
Papaya
Kiwis
Eggplant
Grapefruit
Cantaloupe
Cauliflower
Sweet potatoes

The Dirty Dozen Plus Three

Fruits and vegetables that retain the
most pesticides, with the worst at the
top of the list:

Apples
Peaches
Nectarines
Strawberries
Grapes
Celery
Spinach
Bell peppers
Cucumbers
Cherry tomatoes
Snap peas (imported)
Potatoes
Hot peppers
Kale
Collard Greens

— from the Environmental Working Group's
2015 "Shopper's Guide to Pesticides in
Produce." EWG has updated its guide every
year since 2004. See ewg.org.

system so you can determine just how the produce has been grown. A five-digit code that starts with a 9 means the item is organic. A four-digit code beginning with a 3 or a 4 means the produce is probably conventionally grown.

At the Spiral House, we attempt to eat organically as much as possible, but we understand this may be difficult for some people. Organic foods can cost more than their conventional counterparts because of the farming techniques and fair trade practices that often go hand in hand with them. They may also appear less than perfect due to the lack of pesticide use, but we find these flaws reassuring. They remind us how the foods were grown. After eating organic foods for a while, don't be surprised if those conventionally-grown waxed cucumbers and apples, and dayglow oranges begin to alarm you.

A recent study indicates that people who buy organic have lower levels of organophosphate insecticides measured in their bodies even though they eat more produce than people who buy mostly conventionally-grown fruits and vegetables. If you are not able to buy organic for whatever reason, or need to choose which things to buy organic and which to skip, consider using the Environmental Working Group's ratings as a resource when shopping; see their tips at left.

Fermentation

Originally a method of preserving food, fermentation is almost as old as civilization itself. More recently, we have also learned that it can dramatically aid digestion. During fermentation, bacteria and yeast feed on the natural sugars in foods. As these microorganisms are creating compounds that help to preserve food, they are also adding the kinds of friendly organisms that are touted in probiotic products. Since the gut is the largest component of our immune systems, there is a growing belief that introducing friendly bacteria to our digestive tracts may help to prevent inflammation, allergies, autoimmune illnesses, skin issues, and other conditions in the body as a whole.

There are a slew of fermented plant-based foods available today — dairy-free yogurts, kefirs, and sour creams among them. Miso, a thick paste and traditional Japanese staple, is produced by fermenting soybeans with salt and the fungus *Aspergillus oryzae;* it is used for soup stock, dressings, spreads, and pickling. Of course, vegetables can also be fermented. Turning cabbage into sauerkraut or kimchi (a popular Korean side dish) increases glucosinolate compounds that scientists now believe may fight cancer. Before you fill your fridge with pickles, however, remember that not all fermented foods contain beneficial probiotics, and high levels of salt and sugar may have been added. As with anything, read the label before using.

Egg substitutes

Eggs provide binding, moisture, and leavening. Diane's main substitutions are flax or chia seed (for binding); applesauce or puréed pumpkin (for moisture); and baking powder, baking soda, and yeast (for leavening). Her basic flax egg recipe is: 1 flax egg = 1 tablespoon golden flaxseed soaked in 3 tablespoons warm water for 5 minutes. If you like, you can froth the mixture in a mini food processor. (Diane doesn't; some of us do.) "I haven't yet found anything that adds volume to dishes as well as eggs but I'm working on it," she says, adding, "There's a reason we don't have vegan soufflés or light, fluffy cakes." But even if you find yourself forgoing soufflés, rest assured you will be getting the benefits of healthy omega-3 fatty acids from the flax.

Potatoes

Our old friend, the spud, is a complex carbohydrate that's low in calories — as long as you don't deep-fry or slather it with fatty creams and butters — and a good source of vitamin C and potassium. One medium potato contains 16 percent of the daily recommended amount of fiber and 35 percent of

Our Favorite Edible Flowers
We grow these to use in salads and as garnishes:
   Stella de oro daylily
   Nasturtiums
   Scarlet runner bean blossoms
And we grow these to dry, to use all year long as garnishes and to fill little jam jars to add to our holiday baskets:
   Calendula
   Bachelor Buttons (mostly for color)
   Stella de oro
   Rose petals
Not all parts of all flowers are edible, and some are actually poisonous. Violas, violets, scarlet runner beans, and honeysuckle are entirely edible. With some you should eat the petals only, including calendula, roses, lavender, and chrysanthemums. With the exception of violas and pansies, the sepals (the outer part, usually leafy green, that encloses the flower bud) do not taste good and should be avoided. With all flowers, the stamens and styles (the reproductive parts inside the flower) should be removed before eating because they can detract from the flavor of the food and even cause allergies. So you do need to know what you are eating.

Roasted or steamed? When you wrap a potato or sweet potato in foil, you are steaming it rather than roasting it. Diane bakes her unwrapped potatoes directly on an oven rack. You can place a baking sheet on the rack below to catch drippings, if there are any.

Gluten-free friendly
Most of the recipes in this book are gluten-free. But if a recipe calls for bread or pasta, we assume you will choose one with the ingredients appropriate for your diet. If a recipe calls for flour, and we do not specify a gluten-free flour, then we have not tested the recipe with a gluten-free flour. Gluten-free baking is, itself, a challenge, and even more so when using only plant-based ingredients. "We've had our share of flops," Diane moans. "Don't be afraid to experiment because new flour substitutes are becoming available all the time."

the daily recommended amount of vitamin C. And one baked potato with its skin offers a whopping 1,000 mg. of potassium (the flesh alone contains 600 mg.) as compared with a typical four-ounce banana that has only 422 mgs. but is often touted as one of the best potassium sources. What kind of potato to use in different preparations is the question, however.

- For baking: Choose a russet or Idaho for the large size, thick skin, and starchy, fluffy texture.
- For frying: Baking potatoes make crispy fries.
- For potato pancakes: Again, you want the starch content of the baking potatoes, which helps hold the pancake together.
- For mashing: Diane likes the color and creaminess of Yukon golds.
- For salad: New or red skin varieties because they are low in starch, hold their shape, and absorb dressings well. (Assuming the skins are organic, leave them and all their nutrients intact.)
- For soup: Use anything but baking potatoes, which will fall apart when boiled.

Gluten-free cooking and baking

We limit our intake of gluten at the Spiral House, some of us because of allergies and some because a low-gluten diet makes us feel better. Diane creates many of her dishes without wheat, using flours and other products made with chestnuts, chickpeas, quinoa, oats, amaranth, beans, potatoes, millet, and nuts.

If you need a relatively small amount of certain gluten-free flours (oat, quinoa, almond, walnut), you can quickly make some by grinding the source ingredient in a clean electric coffee or spice grinder. This helps minimize the number of flours stored in your refrigerator and helps to ensure freshness. You'll find conflicting opinions in the nutritional literature concerning the use of almond flour; for one thing, it is very high in polyunsaturated fats, and our diets are often already overloaded with those.

Authentic Foods' Multi-Blend Flour (www.authenticfoods.com) is the best gluten-free all-purpose flour we have found, at the time of this book's publication.

Andean Dream quinoa pastas (spaghetti, macaroni, fusilli) are costly but their taste and texture is way better than most other gluten-free brands we've tried. Diane has perfected cold pasta salad, which can get lumpy and sticky when using gluten-free products. Here's her technique:

• Be sure to use enough water (six quarts for one pound of pasta) and bring it to a rolling boil before you add the pasta. This keeps the pasta from sticking to itself and helps maintain the boil after you add the pasta.

• Salt the water well before adding the pasta, at least one teaspoon for each quart of water. Think of the pasta as swimming in the ocean.

• Add some oil to the cooking water — about two tablespoons per pound of pasta — something Diane doesn't do with wheat pasta.

• Drain the pasta and quickly flash cold water over it, being careful not to overly rinse it.

• Spread the pasta on a baking sheet to cool.

• Drizzle it with a little grapeseed oil (a neutral oil with no flavor) or an oil that is compatible with the recipe.

Oils

Choosing appropriate oils for different culinary uses can be daunting, with their range of flavors, good and bad fats, and smoke points, not to mention their wildly varying prices. Here are the oils Chef Diane uses.

When you cook over high heat (sautéing, frying, grilling), chose an oil with a high smoke point instead; Diane uses peanut or canola; or if the temperature isn't too high, she uses grapeseed oil, which has a medium smoke point. For low-heat cooking and uncooked foods like salad dressings, dips, and salsas, use an oil with a low smoke point; Diane most often uses extra-virgin olive oil, or when she wants a neutral flavor, grapeseed oil.

Why salt your water for pasta, rice, and quinoa? Because it makes the pasta taste better! As the pasta (or grain) absorbs the water, the food is flavored from the inside out. That gives you a tasty foundation for your marinara or stroganoff or other delicious sauce. **When do you salt the water?** After it comes to a boil. Not so much because salt affects the cooking time (the effect is insignificant) but because salt can pit your pot. By adding the salt after the water boils, there's not enough oxygen in the water for the chemical reaction that causes the pitting. **How much salt should you use?** For pasta, Diane uses at least one teaspoon per quart. If that sounds like a lot, remember that most of the salt remains in the water. For rice, she uses ¼ to ½ teaspoon of salt per cup of rice. For quinoa, about ¼ teaspoon per cup.

Gluten-free pasta benefits from being spread on a baking sheet and drizzled with oil before saucing.

The smoke point of oil is exactly what the name suggests: the temperature at which the oil begins to smoke. If you heat oil past its smoke point, it will burn and taste bitter; it will also begin to break down and release free radicals, those unstable molecules that are believed to cause many degenerative and age-related diseases. So it's completely contradictory, for example, to choose a good olive oil for its health benefits and then cook with it over high heat, since olive oil has a low smoke point.

• **Olive oil** has one of the highest levels of heart-healthy monounsaturated fatty acids, and it is also rich in antioxidants. The various grades of olive oil are set by the International Council on Olive Oil, but there is also a great deal of mislabeling. Extra-virgin olive oil is made from the first cold-pressing of whole olives. It is pure fruit juice, and because olives themselves are so variable in taste, so are the extra-virgin oils made from them. A really good one from a small estate can be as expensive as a good bottle of wine. Drizzle these on food just before serving, or use them in a special dressing. There is also a category of "virgin" olive oil, but it is less frequently found in grocery stores. The label "light olive oil" is a marketing term used to describe the oil's lighter flavor; it has nothing to do with calories, but rather is a signal that the oil has been processed using heat or chemicals. It has a high smoke point but because it is processed using heat or chemicals, we don't use it at the Spiral House. The label "olive oil," without any designation, is often a blend of virgin and refined olive oils, and sometimes other oils as well. Read the label.

• **Grapeseed oil** is very versatile due to its fairly neutral flavor and medium-high smoke point. Because it is great for salad dressings, sautéing, and baking, we use it frequently at the Spiral House.

• **Coconut oil** has an unmistakable, sweetly mellow flavor that makes it perfect for baking, frostings, and sautéing, and use in some vegan dishes as a replacement for butter. Greens cooked in a little coconut oil are a whole new taste experience. It has a medium smoke point, so it is not used for high-heat cooking. Coconut oil is a highly saturated fat, though, and we don't yet know how it may contribute to heart disease. All of the research so far has involved short-term studies on its effect on cholesterol levels. In contrast, olive oil is mainly an unsaturated fat and therefore both lowers LDL (low-density lipoprotein or "bad" cholesterol) and increases HDL (high-density lipoprotein or "good" cholesterol). Because coconut oil has a special HDL-boosting effect, it may be less harmful than its otherwise highly-saturated content would imply.

• **Peanut oil** has a mild flavor popular in Asian cooking. Its high smoke point makes it terrific for deep-frying, roasting, grilling, and lots of other uses.

• **Sesame oil**, also used in Asian cuisine, has a medium-high smoke point and a distinct flavor. Use the light sesame oil for deep-frying and the darker toasted sesame oil for stir-frying, dipping sauces, and salad dressings.

• **Canola oil** is lower in saturated fat than olive oil. It's relatively inexpensive and a good, all-purpose choice when you want an oil with a neutral flavor or a high smoke point. Choose organic expeller-pressed oil to avoid GMOs and processing chemicals.

Nuts

We order nuts in bulk from Sara's food co-op, and store them in the refrigerator or freezer depending on available space. Diane toasts them before use, bringing out the oils and enhancing the flavor. You can use a parchment-lined baking sheet in the oven or a dry pan on top of the stove, depending on the quantity of nuts you're toasting. You will know they are done when they are lightly golden and smell toasty. Set a timer and toss them often; the line between perfectly toasted and burnt happens quickly, especially if your attention is on another part of the meal. Put the nuts aside to cool for a few minutes before using them. Even when Diane has leftover toasted nuts, she retoasts them the next time to heighten their flavors.

"Sugar, Ah Honey Honey…"

The problem with sugar is not so much that it is bad for us but that we eat way too much of it. Sugar contributes to weight gain and tooth decay and can place an excessive burden on the pancreas that may lead to diabetes.

The average American consumes 22 teaspoons of sugar a day, most of it from sodas, candy, baked

Store nuts in the refrigerator or freezer. And to enhance their flavor, toast them before use (see information at left).

Honeybees are essential to the security of our food supply. Cross-pollination helps an estimated 30 percent of the world's crops and 90 percent of our wild plants to thrive. Protecting the honeybees from pesticides is another good reason to include as much organically-raised food in your diet as you can.

goods, and cereals. Researchers have found that Americans whose diets are highest in added sugar — those whose daily sugar intake comes to about 500 calories, as opposed to those at the lower end of the research spectrum who take in 160 calories daily from sugar (10 teaspoons) — are twice as likely to die from heart disease.

As an animal product, **honey** is controversial among vegans; some will eat it, others won't. At the Spiral House, we were sufficiently concerned about the collapse of bee colonies that we now have our own beehives on the property. We know the bees are cared for humanely, and so we do eat their honey when they have enough to share with us. We also purchase honey from local beekeepers, who treat their hives respectfully. If you can find honey from the growing number of backyard beekeepers, you will be contributing to the protection of these fascinating and essential creatures. Many allergy sufferers also believe that locally produced honey can mitigate symptoms because the bees carry pollen spores that are transmitted to the honey, helping to build immunity.

Raw sugar We do use various raw sugars in desserts, including white (also called granulated), brown, and turbinado. There's not a whole lot of difference, healthwise, in terms of sugars; the body converts them all to glucose. **White (granulated) sugar** is beet or cane sugar that has been processed, allowed to crystalize, and dried to prevent clumping. **Brown sugar** is basically refined white sugar that has had molasses added back to it. **Turbinado sugar** has been partially processed with some of the molasses remaining. Turbinado is good for sweetening beverages, although it takes longer to dissolve. It can impart a crunchy texture to some baked goods but is not generally used for baking. Diane will choose it for a rub (because it doesn't burn like brown sugar), or sprinkle it on top of cookies and cakes.

For non-dessert dishes requiring a little sweetener, Diane prefers pure, organic **maple syrup** — in granola, some dressings, and certain recipes — because it adds flavor and nutrition along with sweetness. It is rich in nutrients such as manganese, zinc, thiamine, and calcium as well as recently-discovered compounds that have been shown to play key roles in human health like fighting diabetes, cancer, and bacterial illnesses. As with any plant-based food, look for organic brands from small-scale producers who practice sustainable methods.

Molasses is a by-product of refining sugarcane or sugar beets into sugar. It contains iron and a number of essential minerals as well as B vitamins. It is believed to provide relief from menstruation-related problems, obesity, diabetes, stress, cancer-enlarged prostate, acne, and anemia. We have molasses — and Diane — to thank for her Smoky Baked Beans (page 182) and her Molasses Cookies (page 214).

Agave, a natural sweetener with a pleasant neutral taste, is quickly declining in popularity and we no longer use it. While it ranks relatively low on the glycemic index, this is because of its high fructose content, even higher than that of high fructose corn syrup. Fructose doesn't readily raise blood sugar (glucose levels) because it is not well metabolized by the body, but research now indicates that excessive fructose consumption impairs liver function, promotes obesity, and can lead to type 2 diabetes.

Freezing

For those of us living in cold climates, eating locally means putting food by during our short growing season. A well-stocked freezer can also help us get home-cooked meals on the table, even during the busiest times. Some things in the Spiral House freezer are common in food-savvy households. Others might surprise you:

• Whole uncooked tomatoes in freezer bags for use in soups, stews, and sauces. Hold the frozen tomato under hot water for a minute; the skin

Diane's prepared items that freeze well and are great to have on hand include:
• Nutty Parm (page 241)
• Artisanal Feta and Ricotta "Cheeses" (page 18) served as an appetizer, as shown above, or added to other dishes
• Oven-Dried Tomatoes (page 243)

will peel right off. For ease of chopping and good results, chop frozen tomatoes before they are fully defrosted.

- Oven-Dried Tomatoes (page 243), home grown and home dried, then placed in freezer bags.
- Rhubarb stalks, cut into two- to three-inch lengths, frozen raw, if for no other reason than to make Diane's Cauliflower, Red Lentil, and Rhubarb Dal (page 144) in the winter.
- Blanched vegetables from summer's bounty — all the cooking greens; peas; asparagus; broccoli; and beans, including runner, French, dwarf, and broad varieties.
- Fruits, also from our garden, including strawberries, blueberries, raspberries, and peaches. To prepare the fruit for freezing, Diane recruits all free hands to hull the strawberries, peel and slice the peaches, and make sure there are no stems on the berries. She then spreads the fruit by type in a single layer on a parchment paper-lined baking sheet and places it in the freezer. Once frozen, she transfers the fruit into freezer bags, labels them, and returns the bags to the freezer.
- Fresh herbs frozen for winter retain more of their fresh flavor than do dried herbs. We chop garden-fresh chives and freeze them in tiny containers. Break off pieces as needed and drop them into soups or other dishes while cooking. We put basil leaves in a single layer on a baking sheet lined with parchment paper and pop the pan in the freezer for a couple of hours. We put the frozen basil in a plastic bag and return it to the freezer for storage. We also love garden guru Margaret Roach's frozen parsley logs, made by packing fresh parsley into the bottom of a freezer bag and then rolling it tightly. To use, remove from the freezer, cut off as much of the log as you need, and return the rest to the freezer.
- A wide variety of prepared foods made from the recipes in this book. Dishes that freeze well are indicated in the Note section for each recipe.

Many of us never thought of freezing **rhubarb**, or of using it in anything other than strawberry-rhubarb pie. But then Diane introduced us to Cauliflower, Lentil, Rhubarb Dal (page 144). It's the first crop we freeze as each new gardening season begins.

• That partial can of leftover coconut milk poured into a small, freezer-proof container.

• Fresh ginger. In addition to extending the shelf life, frozen ginger is easy to grate. (If it's organic, there is no need to peel it). And if you defrost it, you can easily squeeze its juice.

• Cooked rice spread out in freezer bags to a thickness of about one inch. The flat frozen bags are then stored on top of one another to save room.

Always cool foods before you freeze them; then, wrap them well or put them in sealed containers to prevent freezer burn. Remember to label your items with the name and date. We use freezer tape and permanent markers. Don't freeze vegetables with high water content, like cucumbers, lettuce, radishes, and bean sprouts.

When preparing vegetables for freezing, never steam them. Quickly blanch the same variety together in a large pot of water. Scoop them out of the boiling water with a slotted spoon or strainer and place them in ice water until chilled. Drain well on paper towels and scatter the vegetables on a parchment paper-lined baking sheet, let them dry, and place them in the freezer. Once frozen, transfer to a freezer bag or container and label.

Storage

Some years back, researchers at the University of Arizona collaborated with the U.S. Department of Agriculture to track the food-use habits of American families. The results were shocking. The families studied, threw away an average of 470 pounds of food each year, about 14 percent of all the food they brought into their homes. They did this at an annual cost to themselves of some $600 per family. Nationally, Americans dump an estimated $43 billion worth of food every year, most of it because it has spoiled.

If your produce is rotting, you may be storing incompatible fruits and veggies together. Those that give off high levels of ethylene gas, a ripening

We fill our **freezer bags** so that they can lie flat. So instead of getting maximum capacity out of each bag, we have bags that stack efficiently on top of one another in the freezer.

agent, will lead ethylene-sensitive foods to decay. Keep these kinds separate. On the other hand, you can use trapped ethylene to your advantage. Encourage a peach to ripen, for instance, by putting it in a closed paper bag with a ripe banana.

Get a complete chart of chilling with fruits and veggies at www.vegetariantimes.com or elsewhere online and keep it handy in your kitchen because one bad apple really can spoil the whole bunch. A variety of reusable food storage bags that will absorb ethylene are now on the market, such as those by Evert-Fresh and BioFresh.

Some Spiral House Favorites

The degree to which a plant-based diet is becoming mainstream can be measured by the dizzying number of new vegan products, cookbooks, blogs, websites, and organizations devoted to it. As the choices are so numerous, and the results of substituting different products so variable, we opted to share an incomplete, ever-evolving list of favorites.

Food products

Whole and organic foods are no longer limited to health food stores, food co-ops, and one's own chemical-free garden. Many supermarkets now routinely stock organic items. No matter where you shop, though, read the labels. Remember that products can be labeled "natural" and still be loaded with stuff your grandmother never heard of and you can't pronounce. Many of us don't have the first clue about the amount of additives we are consuming. At the Spiral House, we try to forego artificial food colors, sweeteners, preservatives, flavor enhancers (MSG), high-fructose corn syrup, and processed ingredients whenever possible. We look for products labeled free of GMOs. On the following pages, you will find some of the items and companies we use and recommend.

To maximize the taste, aroma, and appearance of fresh herbs, don't over chop them. With large leaves like basil, use the **chiffonade technique**: Stack and roll the leaves, then use a sharp knife to thinly slice them into ribbons. If you want the herbs smaller, slice the strips again in the other direction.

Pasta, grain, and tempeh

• Andean Dream quinoa pastas: They're costly but we are willing to eat less for such a good gluten-free pasta (available at most large health food stores).
• Lightlife wild rice and flax seed tempehs (lightlife.com).
• Native Harvest wild rice (nativeharvest.com).
• 'e Paccheri Lisci: An Italian import made from, rice flour, corn flour, and water, it is not only gluten-free but we think just about the best pasta to be had. (Available in specialty food stores, it's worth asking your favorite store to order it for you.)

Meat analogues

Many commercial meat substitutes are processed and loaded with chemicals and preservatives, which kind of defeats the healthy reasons for eating a plant-based diet. Some analogues are better than others, though, and can help in a pinch when time is short. As with any processed food, read the labels.
• Beyond Meat (beyondmeat.com) is a California-based company that is on a mission to improve health, have a beneficial impact on climate change, and treat animals compassionately, replacing animal protein with plant protein, one meal at a time. Their non-GMO products combine soy and pea protein to produce chicken and beef substitutes. Beyond Meat's Beyond Chicken Lightly Seasoned Strips (see Diane's Better-than-Chicken Salad, page 111) and the company's Beyond Beef Feisty Crumble (which Diane serves mixed with beans in her tacos) are two we find ourselves using on a regular basis.

Other analogues some of us find helpful in our own kitchens include:
• Gardein's mostly vegan products (gardein.com), which include various meatless burgers, sliders, and chicken strips. Read the labels because a few contain dairy.
• Lightlife (lightlife.com) Fakin' Bacon Tempeh Strips
• Trader Joe's Soy "Chorizo" (which happens to be gluten-free).

One of our favorite pastas ('e Paccheri Lisci) happens to be gluten-free and is scrumptuous with Diane's Roasted Garden Marina Sauce (page 230). Available ridged or unridged, these large tubes are also great for stuffing and baking.

Bringing kids into the garden is one of the best ways we've found to help set good eating habits.

Umeboshi Plum Vinegar

Many of us who consider ourselves reasonably serious cooks — and eaters — finally "got" the complexity of umeboshi plum vinegar after realizing it was the common ingredient in some of Diane's dishes: the Spiral House Salad (page 70), Quinoa Tabbouleh (page 93), and Brussels Sprouts and Hijiki (page 88). The plum vinegar is both salty and sweet, fruity and sour, and can make these salads more addictive than potato chips (and a whole lot healthier, too). The taste is a perfect expression of the yin/yang philosophy that is at the heart of the Spiral House. Note, though, that when using umeboshi vinegar you might want to reduce the salt you would otherwise use in a dish.

Dairy substitutes
- Earth Balance Natural Buttery Spread or Sticks
- Earth Balance Vegan Shortening
- Trader Joe's Vegan Cream Cheese Alternative
- Tofutti Better Than Cream Cheese
- Tofutti Sour Cream (not their Sour Supreme product)
- Silk Organic Original Soy Milk
- Silk Cashew Milk
- Blue Diamond Almond Breeze Almond Milk
- Daiya Foods "uncheese" blocks, slices, and shreds (daiyafoods.com) are free of soy and dairy and they melt like the real thing. They don't offer much in the way of nutritive value, though, so use them judiciously.
- Hampton Creek's Just Mayo
- Follow Your Heart Organic Vegenaise (a Spiral House staple until Diane discovered Just Mayo)

Oils
- Zoe Organic Extra Virgin Olive Oil
- La Tourangelle Expeller-Pressed Grapeseed Oil
- Kadoya Toasted Sesame Oil

Seasonings and condiments
- Celtic salt
- Himalayan pink salt (fine) by Artisan
- Red Star nutritional yeast
- Bragg Liquid Aminos is not fermented (for those on special diets), is gluten-free, and is made from non-GMO soybeans. As such, it is an excellent alternative for tamari and soy sauce.
- The Wizards Organic Vegan Worcestershire
- Annie's Homegrown and Organic Vegan Worcestershire
- Bragg Organic Apple Cider Vinegar
- Frank's Red Hot sauce
- Sriracha-style hot chili sauce
- Pickapeppa Sauce
- Ariston Balsamic Vinegar
- Eden Umeboshi Plum Vinegar

Shortcuts

Even the best chefs keep some convenience foods in the pantry, and these are ones Diane especially likes:

• Bob's Red Mill Gluten-Free Pizza Crust Mix: This makes a good focaccia base for simple toppings like caramelized onions, our homemade feta cheese, and olives. Once it's on our plates, some of us will add other items from the assortment Diane puts out. She doesn't use it for a traditional round pizza pie, however.

• Tarazi Falafel Mix

• Frontera New Mexico Taco Skillet Sauce

• Trader Joe's line of "10 minute cooking" items: farro, barley, and lentils

Et Cetera

• Any good Italian canned tomato; we opt for San Marzanos. ("You get what you pay for when you buy canned tomatoes," Diane believes. "Buy a good tomato and you get a good tomato.")

• Pacific Foods Organic Vegetable Broth

• Trader Joe's Organic Vegetable Broth

• Trader Joe's Miso Ginger Broth

• Maine Coast organic seaweeds (There's less concern about their exposure to radiation pollution.)

• Dried heirloom beans (and posole) from Rancho Gordo (ranchogordo.com)

• Smoked salt: Use in rubs for grilled vegetables, in baked beans, or anything with a barbeque flavor. You can control the intensity more than with liquid smoke. There are many brands; be sure to check the label to be certain it doesn't include any ingredients you want to avoid.

Sous chef Valerie Augustine. That's her son, Tanyon, on the facing page. And did we mention that Val is engaged to Diane's son, Kevin Vines, who was part of the original construction crew at the Spiral House and is head of Tom's sculpture crew?

Kitchen Equipment

It is so easy to get carried away with kitchen equipment. In a moment of rare restraint, we offer our short list of essentials:

• Diane prefers cast-iron, enamel-coated cast-iron, glass, or ceramic cookware. We tend to use parchment paper in lieu of nonstick cookware (see caption, below left).

• The best set of knives you can afford

• A good food processor

• A mini food processor

• Immersion blender: This wand-like tool lets you purée soup directly in the pot in which it was cooked. It is inexpensive and saves the time and cleanup of transferring soups and sauces from pot to blender.

• Microplane grater: For finely grating lemon, orange, and ginger.

• A stovetop grill pan: The cast-iron style we use fits flat on the stovetop over two burners, allowing you to grill indoors without the vegetables or other items sitting in oil.

• A good-size mortar and pestle: Great for grinding spices and for those occasions when you want the subtlety of a pesto or other sauce made by hand rather than in the blender.

• Paderno World Cuisine A4982799 Tri-Blade spiralizer: What's a Spiral House without a Spiral Salad (page 70).

• Vitamix Classic 5200 Standard Blender: This high-powered blender is pricey, but if you can swing it, it's very useful for making smoothies, sauces, cashew and nut milks, nut and grain flours, and a zillion other things your lower-powered blender will struggle to turn out. (Less expensive brands are available.)

• Rice cooker: When there is a lot going on in the kitchen and the meal includes plain cooked rice, Diane likes to use a rice cooker. The rice comes out perfectly and you don't have to watch it.

• Pressure cooker: If you need beans cooked quickly (say in a third of the time needed to simmer them on

Parchment paper can be used in baking as a disposable, nonstick surface. It also has good heat resistance that generally allows it to tolerate oven temperatures of up to 425 degrees. (Check your brand's instructions just to be sure.)

the stovetop), a pressure cooker is invaluable. Also, any food that you cook in a pressure cooker retains more nutrients than it would cooked some other way.

Tidbits

• Why do we roast vegetables for use in our sauces and stocks? For depth of flavor. Roasting the vegetables at 350 degrees for almost an hour will caramelize them, intensifying their flavors. Then if you deglaze the pan with a little water, white wine, or Bragg Liquid Aminos, you can scrape every bit of goodness into the stockpot.

• When chopping garlic, after you chop a little, sprinkle with some salt — this will keep the garlic from sticking to the knife.

• After you boil beets, run them under cold water and the skin will come right off.

• When you cook lentils, don't add too much salt to the water or they will split and get mushy.

• Always buy super-fresh nuts and seeds and store them in the fridge. Peanuts and peanut butter can harbor molds. Select organic ones only and purchase them fresh and in small quantities.

• Send us your favorite kitchen tips and we'll collect them on our website (4goodness-sake.com).

Buy the best **knives** you can afford, learn the nuances of basic knife techniques, keep them sharp, and care for them well. You'll have them forever.

Sources for Kitchen Wisdom

Organic labeling See the federal Food and Drug Administration's website *www.ams.usda.gov/grades-standards/organic-standards*

Protein requirements Physicians Committee for Responsible Medicine: *www.pcrm.org/health/diets/vegdiets/how-can-i-get-enough-protein-the-protein-myth*

Sugar American Heart Association: www.heart.org

Nutritional composition of foods United States Department of Agriculture's National Nutrient Database, *http://ndb.nal.usda.gov/*, ignoring the animal products.

Sources for Kitchen Wisdom continues on page 272

Fermentation

Tufts University newsletter: www.nutritionletter.tufts.edu/issues/10_2/current-articles/Discover-the-Digestive-Benefits-of-Fermented-Foods_1383-1.html

Fermentation Essentials: The Essential Guide for Fermentation and Probiotic Foods, by Sandi Lane, an inexpensive ebook from Barnes and Noble (2015)

DIY Fermentation: Over 100 Step-by-Step Home Fermentation Recipes, by Rockridge Press (Calisto Media, 2015), an easy book for beginners.

Gluten-free cooking and baking *Great Gluten-Free Vegan Eats* by Allyson Kramer (Fair Winds Press, 2012).

Cooking oils For olive oil standards, health facts, and recipes, visit the International Olive Council, internationaloliveoil.org/

Produce storage *Vegetarian Times, Spoiled Rotten, How to Store Fruits and Vegetables*: www.vegetariantimes.com/

Sources for Why Plant-Based

Health

Learn more about the health aspects of a plant-based diet at the website of the Physicians Committee for Responsible Medicine (*www.pcrm.org*).

For information on obesity, visit the federal Center For Disease Control's website: www.cdc.gov/obesity/data/adult.html) and People for the Ethical Treatment of Animals' website (*www.peta.org*).

The ground-breaking China-Cornell-Oxford Project found that Chinese people who lived in areas with high meat consumption were more likely to die of so-called Western illnesses such as cancer, heart disease, diabetes, and obesity than Chinese people from parts of China where the diet was more plant-based. For more information, read, *The China Study: The Most Comprehensive Study of Nutrition Ever Conducted and the Startling Implications for Diet*, by T. Colin Campbell and Thomas Campbell (BenBella Books, 2006).

The Environment

An attention-getting 2006 United Nations report titled *Livestock's Long Shadow* found livestock production accounts for 18 percent of all greenhouse gas emissions, more than that produced by all forms of transportation combined.

Eight percent of global human water use is now devoted to raising animals for food with most of it going to the animals' feed crops, according to the not-for-profit Council for Agriculture, Science and Technology: www.*cast-science.org/publications*

The United States Department of Agriculture estimates that it takes about fifteen pounds of feed to make one pound of beef, six pounds of feed for one pound of pork, and five pounds of feed for one pound of chicken.

Researchers at the University of Chicago concluded that switching from a standard American diet to a vegan diet is more effective than switching from a conventional car to a hybrid when it comes to the fight against climate change. (*The Huffington Post*, April 22, 2014, (www.huffingtonpost.com).

Humane Issues

Eating Animals, by Jonathan Safran Foer (Little, Brown and Company, 2009).

Farm Sanctuary: Changing Heart and Minds About Animals and Food, by Gene Baur (Simon & Schuster, 2008).

RESOURCES

Vegan Organizations

• People for the Ethical Treatment of Animals (**Peta.org**). Request their free vegan starter kit and information on transitioning to a vegan lifestyle. They offer lots of other useful information as well. Be forewarned that they are a no-holds-barred political action organization.

• The Vegetarian Resource Group (**vrg.org**) is a good first stop for vegan information — recipes, diet, ethical considerations, lifestyle tips, advice on raising vegan children, and more.

• Physicians Committee for Responsible Medicine (**pcrm.org**) combines the clout and expertise of more than 12,000 physicians with the dedicated actions of 150,000 members around the world. The organization supports doctors in empowering their patients to take control of their own health, as well as bringing nutrition into medical education and practice. The organization also works tirelessly for alternatives to the use of animals in medical education and research in an effort to shift research from animal models to human-relevant studies.

Websites and Blogs

You'll find a wealth of information about the plant-based diet and lifestyle on the Internet. Two starting points:

• Happy Cow (**Happycow.net**) lists vegan- and vegan-friendly restaurants in just about every major city in the world. It's a great resource for finding delicious, whole, and humane food when traveling or even at home.

• VegNews (**Vegnews.com**) is a vibrant vegan magazine bursting with news, lifestyle articles, recipes, shopping and beauty ideas, travel and ecology info, all with the intent of making animal-free and ethical living easier. And fun.

Blogs: There are new ones all the time. Is there a better reason for Google?

• Kris Carr, the best-selling author (*Crazy Sexy Kitchen*, *Crazy Sexy Diet*, and *Crazy Sexy Juice*), wellness activist, and cancer survivor has been instrumental in making the plant-based diet accessible, exciting and, yes, sexy. Her website (**kriscarr.com**) will link you to a variety

of themed blogs sure to cheer you and have you replacing conventional dishes with recipes like Soba Noodle Salad with Mango, Red Pepper, and Cashews in no time.

• My New Roots (**mynewroots.org**) and the eponymous cookbook by holistic nutritionist Sarah Britton are new favorites of some of us at the Spiral House. Her diet is 99% vegan, her recipes and entire site are inspirational, and the photography is luscious.

• Oh She Glows (**ohsheglows.com**), again both a blog and a cookbook, was started by vegan superstar Angela Liddon as a vehicle to help her recover from an eating disorder. Nearly a decade later, she is the picture of robust health, the book is a bestseller, and the award-winning blog boasts well over 1 million unique visitors monthly. Count many of us among them.

• Post Punk Kitchen (**theppk.com**) is the popular blog by Isa Chandra Moscowitz, co-author of the vegan classic *Veganomicon*. If you're a newbie, the videos on her site will help you "Make It Vegan."

• Eat Good Food (**allysonkramer.com**) by Allyson Kramer specializes in a wide variety of gluten-free vegan recipes with many tailored for individuals with multiple food allergies. And the photography is to die for. At least to cook for.

• Deliciously Ella (**deliciouslyella.com**) is the website of Ella Woodward, who ate her way back to health after dealing with a relatively rare illness, postural tachycardia syndrome. Her bestselling books, *Deliciously Ella* and *Deliciously Ella Every Day*, and her blog, available through her website, will inspire you to change your diet without feeling deprived and help you embrace a healthier style of life.

• Hudson Valley Seed Library (**seedlibrary.org**), both a certified organic farm and a certified organic seed handler, offers heirloom and open-pollinated seeds for vegetable, flower, and herb varieties — many of them produced on their own Hudson Valley, New York-based farm. The rest are sourced from other local farmers, farmers in other regions, and from trustworthy wholesale seed houses. They offer great tips on the use of row covers, among many, many other things.

• Garden guru Margaret Roach's blog, **awaytogarden.com**, takes its name from the eponymous book she wrote in 1998, chosen as best book of that year by the Garden Writers Association of America and now a collector's item. The former garden editor at both *Newsday* and at *Martha Stewart Living*, she offers seasonal advice, especially for those in the Northeast, that is invaluable.

Farm Animal Sanctuaries

These not-for-profit organizations seek to educate the public about how factory farms treat farm animals. The groups promote compassionate vegan living, offer internships and opportunities for volunteering with the animals they have rescued, and are open for regular tours. They are great places to take kids and houseguests. Some operate bed and breakfasts so you can have a farm vacation, getting up close and personal with animals that will become your friends, not your food. Many run summer camps for children and even vegan cooking classes. The three below in upstate New York are the ones we wholeheartedly support. Find one in your area that is accredited by the Global Federation of Animal Sanctuaries (sanctuaryfederation.org) and get involved. You will find it rewarding beyond words.

• **Catskill Animal Sanctuary** (casanctuary. org), 316 Old Stage Rd., Saugerties, NY 12477, (845) 336-8447.

• **Woodstock Farm Animal Sanctuary** (woodstocksanctuary.org), 2 Rescue Rd., High Falls, NY 12447, (845) 247-5700. (This is their new, more animal- and neighbor-friendly location.)

• **Farm Sanctuary** (farmsanctuary.org), 3100 Aikens Rd., (PO Box 150 for mail service), Watkins Glen, NY 14891. Founded in 1986, it was America's first shelter for farm animals.

ACKNOWLEDGMENTS

Any list of those who lent support to our *For Goodness Sake* endeavor must begin with Patty Livingston and Tom Gottsleben, who have opened their home and hearts to those in their employ, making our work at the Spiral House so much more than just jobs. The love and kindness they show everyone around them on a daily basis is inspirational and formed the nurturing environment out of which this book and other projects were born. Their commitment to compassionate living and spiritual self-discovery has motivated many of us to make changes in our own lives. It has long been their idea and hope to produce a Spiral House vegan cookbook.

Thanks also to Hudson Valley photographers Mick Hales and Phil Mansfield, two outstanding artists with numerous credits to their names, who contributed photos of Tom's sculpture and the Spiral House that were taken for an upcoming book on the Spiral House's creation. Their vision added layers of color and meaning to our work.

Cookbook author/editor Sarah Scheffel, a friend from vegan and humane circles, stepped in at the eleventh hour to provide a thorough and scrupulous editing of pages that we had all looked at way too many times by then. She saved us from ourselves on more than one occasion.

Jennie Brown, co-founder of the Woodstock Farm Animal Sanctuary (woodstocksanctuary. org); Kathy Stevens, founder of the Catskill Animal Sanctuary (casanctuary.org); and best-selling cookbook author, wellness advocate, and cancer survivor Kris Carr (kriscarr.com), read the first incarnation of our book and offered early praise and endorsements that have been helpful in so many ways. Thanks to all of you. We have so much respect for your work.

Electrician/carpenter Chris Stralka, a key member of Tom Gottsleben's crew, built a special tabletop for the food shoots that proved indispensable and helped many of the book's images to convey the warmth and relaxed mood at our shared meals. Thanks to Chris also for our amazing raised beds in the vegetable gardens with copper rims to deter the slugs. And for our garlic drying rack. And so much more.

We would also like to thank ceramic artists Elena Zang and Alan Hoffman and potter/sculptor Stephen Fabrico for the use of their exquisite dishes for many of our photo shoots. Their creativity sparked ours.

Crystal Star, our indomitable and talented Photoshop artist, worked her pixel magic on digital minutiae that had caused our eyes to cross. She always amazes us.

Jane Polcovar and Sara Gast, who know our garden like their own: Jane was Diane's recipe scribe, and Sara was a mainstay in the kitchen on "cookbook days." Thank you both, not just for your expertise, but also for your generous spirits.

Carie Salberg and Anjali Bermain, our beloved garden angels, were always there when we needed a helping hand. Carie managed much of the garden's care during the final stages of editing and production and Anjali picked up her camera when Andrea needed to be in the photos herself (pages 210–211). Thank you darlings.

Maria Santamaria, office manager at the Spiral House, was our go-to person for more tasks than we could list. Whether we needed a domain name, bar code, copyright information, presentation materials, even lunch on Diane's days off, Maria always took care of it, and always unflappably. Thank you Maria for being you.

Chrissy Deibert, owner of The Copy Hut in Kingston, New York, printed an early "teaser" version of this book, providing quality printing and technical support that helped guide us from that early effort to the book you are holding.

Jay Kreider, our indexer, knows just how to make a book easier to use so that whatever you are looking for is right at your fingertips, literally.

Carol Frazzetta, Diane's first formal cooking instructor, inspired in her the desire and confidence to cook professionally, for which our gratitude equals Diane's. Without the training and wisdom Diane gained in Carol's kitchen, we would not have had Chef Diane and her years of professional experience to create the recipes in this book.

At Worzalla, our state-of-the-art printer in Stevens Point, Wisconsin, Tim Taylor, our account representative, exhibited limitless patience with our requests for samples and our ruthlessness about details until the very end. Lisa Ceplina, our Customer Service Rep, moved us through production effortlessly. In the technical department, Worzalla's Kitty Grigsby and Brian Mallon helped us get our minds around oh so many things we needed to know to produce the beautiful book you are holding. Thank you.

And, finally, our thanks to Book Publishing Company, a community-owned press based in Summertown, Tennessee, dedicated to publishing books that promote a healthy and sustainable lifestyle. They understood what we were about immediately and supported our vision of community, compassionate living, and sustainability, which also proved to be theirs. Bob Holzapfel, the company's president, and his group there have been encouraging, professional, and fun. And we love to have fun. For Goodness Sake!

WWW.4GOODNESS-SAKE.COM

Enjoying this book? Then join us on the continuing journey: Visit the Spiral House blog at 4Goodness-Sake.com, and sign up for our e-newsletter. The blog features articles, luscious photos, and tips about the vegan lifestyle and all it encompasses. Our recipes cover the spectrum from 30-minute meals to exquisite culinary creations for parties and holidays. We'll get down and dirty about what's growing in our organic garden that might be perfect for yours, and keep you posted on the state of honey bees, pending humane legislation, and other important social, environmental, and food-related issues. You'll also find lots of health ideas, new products, and, of course, the lowdown on happenings here in the Spiral House community, including what makes us laugh. That's something we love to do because it keeps us happy, healthy, and sane. Here's a taste of things to come:

• We're going shopping with chef Diane Hagedorn to report on some of her favorite plant-based and gluten-free products at Trader Joe's, Whole Foods, and our local health food store.
• Why you don't need to be afraid of pressure cookers. Diane will demystify these contraptions so you can prepare food more quickly and healthily.
• The coming season's seed order, what's tried-and-true and what's new.
• Why we love lemon verbena, and how we grow it, dry it, and bag it in muslin teabags to give away in decorative tins during the December holidays.
• Growing microgreens, previewed at right.
We hope you'll join us at the blog and share some of your own experiences and ideas.

Microgreens All Year Long: From Seed to Table in 10 to 14 Days

Did you know these tiniest of greens pack a hugely healthful wallop? You've seen them as garnishes in fine restaurants, where chefs like to use the delicate young plants to enhance the presentation and taste of their soups, salads, entrées, and sandwiches. They are available commercially but need to be fresh-cut from a germination tray to preserve their flavors and texture. How much better then to grow your own, an option that will give you a steady and inexpensive supply.

You can grow them indoors just about anywhere, from the basement to a corner of the kitchen. All you need to get started is a germination tray, some potting soil, organic vegetable seeds suitable for microgreens — broccoli is our enduring favorite — and a florescent grow light to provide a steady and even supply of light for about 12 hours per day. Or do what we did and get fancy with a 3-Tier SunLite Garden from Gardener's Supply Company (gardeners.com). That way, you can start your garden seedlings side by side with your microgreens. Needless to say, there are many cost and space options in between, including peat pots in a sunny window.

The most important requirements are bright, full-spectrum lights and healthy organic seeds. We buy our seeds from Sprout People (sproutpeople.org). Your full-spectrum florescent lights, germination trays, and organic potting soil (either soil or peat-based) are available at any large garden center. Pick up a standard shop light fixture at your local hardware or building supply store. A timer is helpful so you don't have to turn the lights off and on.

The best seeds for growing microgreens are salad greens, leafy vegetables, and herbs. Once you have the hang of it, consider growing a few different types at the same time in different trays because of the different germination times. Beware of seed mixes from suppliers for this reason. You can create your own "house" mix after harvesting. There are lots of greens to choose from: arugula, basil, beets, broccoli, cilantro, cress, dill, flax, kale, mizuna, mustard, peas, purple or daikon radish, and tatsoi, just to name a few. They are best purchased from a microgreen seed supplier so you can buy in the bulk you will need. The little seed packs at your garden center won't cut it.

So what's the reason for our love affair with microgreens? Unlike sprouts, which are grown in water, microgreens are grown in soil and eaten as soon as the fully developed stems and leaves appear, generally about 10 to 14 days after planting. A study done at the University of Maryland in College Park in 2012 found that microgreens were four- to 40-times more concentrated with nutrients than their mature counterparts. They are extremely high in vitamins, minerals, and enzymes; in other words, a very little goes a very long way. You'll have a tough time finding a food that is fresher.

Photos, below top row: To grow microgreens, place an inch or two of moistened soil on the bottom of a germination tray, generously scatter your seeds evenly over the soil, press down lightly, and cover with a thin layer of soil. Moisten the soil with a mister and mist once or twice daily with a spray bottle. *Bottom row:* When your microgreens have their first leaves, they are ready to eat. With a clean scissors, cut them close to the soil level, using the tip of the scissors to trim away or scrape off any loose soil that adheres to the greens.

Tom Gottsleben was born in Milwaukee, Wisconsin, and educated in Japan, at the San Francisco Art Institute, and in an Indian ashram. His sculpture creates for the viewer an experience of the harmony and beauty inherent in nature's patterns and in the union of what appear to be opposites — linear and curved, light and dark, form and void, and many others. Informed by both science and mysticism, Tom's work inspires us to look more closely, to be more engaged, and to be available for the wonder that presents itself at every turn.

His work has been the subject of solo exhibitions at the Neuberger Museum of Art (Purchase, NY), the Museum at Bethel Woods (Bethel, NY), Art Omi International (Ghent, NY), and in group shows at the annual Contemporary Sculpture at Chesterwood (Stockbridge, MA) and The New York Botanical Garden (Bronx, NY). His work is in numerous private collections and is represented by Elena Zang Gallery, Shady (Woodstock, NY).

For more information, contact
Elena Zang Gallery
ezang@hvc.rr.com
845-679-5432
www.elenazang.com
www.tomgottsleben.com

The cookbook team sitting on a spiral wall that Tom created. Center front: Chef Diane Hagedorn Left to right: Rocky, Andrea, Ronnie, Jane, Patty, Tom, Sara, and Val.

The Cookbook Team

Patty Livingston and Tom Gottsleben • Publishers and Inspirations
Diane Hagedorn • Chef Extraordinaire
Andrea Barrist Stern • Photographer, Food Stylist, and Co-editor
Ronnie Shushan • Graphic Designer and Co-editor
Val Augustine • Sous Chef and Recipe Reviewer
Jane Polcovar • Recipe Scribe, Garden and Kitchen Crew
Sara Gast • Garden and Kitchen Crew

The creative genius behind the recipes in this book, **Diane Hagedorn** was raised in a home where there was always a bounty of food on the table, all of it prepared by a mother who never used recipes. After moving to New York's Hudson Valley with her family in the early 1980s, Diane studied at the renowned Culinary Institute of America for three years. She went on to serve as the chef at numerous area restaurants, including those at retreat centers and resorts.

When she started cooking at the Spiral House — first at holiday parties and special events related to Tom's artwork, and then eventually as the property's full-time chef — Diane began to veganize her repertoire. And so we have plant-based versions of the comfort food she grew up on, the Italian food her kids loved, the New Orleans food she craves from her many visits there, and the elegant dishes from her restaurant days. She brings an exacting standard to all of her cooking, and still somehow remembers everyone's individual favorites.

Andrea Barrist Stern is a photographer and journalist living just outside Woodstock, New York. As a long-time newspaper reporter and editor, both her photography and her reporting have been honored with awards from the New York Press Association and other organizations. She also now wears the hat of head gardener at the Spiral House property, where organics prevail, from the seed and soil to gardening techniques and pest control. In photographing this book she avoided the dyes, preservatives, and fixatives commonly used in contemporary food photography. For goodness sake, what you see is what you will eat.

INDEX

Cooking is love made visible.
— Anonymous

For Goodness Sake collects the wisdom
that an eclectic circle of friends, artists, and
professionals have acquired about the food
they share each day. Chef Diane Hagedorn
prepares the group's meals in the kitchen of
the Spiral House — a unique stone structure
based on sacred geometry in New York's
Hudson Valley that was designed by artist
Tom Gottsleben.

The recipes selected here from those
vegan meals include comfort foods, elegant
party fare, holiday favorites, ethnic cuisines,
and dishes made with some of the best new
plant-based substitutes for animal products.
Most are gluten-free.

For Goodness Sake will appeal to anyone
who likes delicious food: vegans, vegetarians,
and meat eaters who want to expand their
vegetable repertoire.